AFRICAN COSMOLOGY OF THE BANTU-KONGO

Principles of Life & Living

African Cosmology of the Bantu Kongo

ISBN: 1-59232-463-0

Reprint Edition

African Tree Press

Diâdi nza-Kôngo kandongila: Mono i kadi kia dingo-dingo (kwènda-vutukisa) kinzungidila ye didi dia ngolo zanzîngila. Ngiena, kadi yateka kala ye kalulula ye ngina vutuka kala ye kalulula.

Here is what the Kongolese Cosmology taught me: I am going-and-coming-back-being around the center of vital forces. I am because I was and re-was before, and that I will be and re-be again.

Contents

Introduction to the First Edition

Malèmbe!

This work was written for my seminar discussions at Yale University in 1980. I also wanted it to be a book for everybody which is why I decided to call it *The African Book Without Title.*

If either a lawyer, an anthropologist, a philosopher, an educator, a politician, a linguist, a diplomat, a therapist or an ordinary man can find in this work anything that may be useful to their field, then let them call the book the way they want it to be called in order to fit it into their field.

Africans, including those of African descent, must love the study of their languages if they wish to talk honestly about themselves and about what they are, for all systems' codes of their society are coded (tied) in these languages [makolo mamo ma bimpa bia kimvuka kiâu makângwa mu ndînga zôzo]. These languages should be studied and used as languages of instruction in order to prove their scientific capacity [lèndo kiâu kianzâyila].

To study language is the most important process of learning the art of coding and decoding social systems of human society in the world [kinkete kia kânga ye kutula makolo ma fu bia kimvuka kia mûntu mu nza]. Learning is an accumulative process of coding and decoding cultures, therefore, it is necessary to study the language that expresses those cultures—[longuka i nzila yangyumbikila ku nsia n'kîngu wa nkângulu ye nkutudulu a makolo manzâyila ma mûntu]. One also has to learn, the art of tying/coding [kin-kete kia kânga] in order to understand the opposite side of that art, how to untie/decode [bwè mu kutula]; only one who understands the codes of their social and conceptual systems can decode them for the outside world. This Kôngo proverb/principle does state: A community's knots/codes are decoded by its members; variant Systems' codes are only decoded by their members [Makolo makânga kânda kutula mwisikânda, variant Makolo makânga kimpa, kutula kimpa/mwisikimpa].

Africanists and all African wisdom lovers, likewise, must be interested in the study of African languages in order to avoid yesterday's biased blunders. How can someone be a true Africanist if he/she is not able to speak a single African language? How could he/she represent a system he/she dares not truly taste and feel? To awakening Africans, such scholars are very dangerous for Africa because they negatively lead the most dangerous exploitation of man by man, the intellectual exploitation. They impose themselves upon others by interpreting negatively other people's ideas, i.e., what they call "their raw materials/their original work." Moreover those ideas are badly understood since they were harvested in a hurry, and all kinds of cultural misrepresentation and fantasies occur in the process of "filling in the blanks."

Food tastes good only if one can taste and feel the mind and heart of the person who cooked it. This applies to cultures as well. A systematic understanding therefore is possible only if one can taste and feel the radiation beauty [n'niènzi a minienie] of the language that generates that culture.

A work, a teaching, a gift, a laugh or an explanation from a violent and bloody mind has a great impact on its consumer. We are what we consume, learn, hear, see and feel. We feel waves/vibrations and radiations [minika ye minienie] because we ourselves produce waves/vibrations and radiations. We are sensitive to heat, cold, and electricity, [tiya, kiôzi ye ngolo za n'cezi/sula] only because we ourselves as organisms produce heat, cold, and electricity.

The American statesman who said that USA citizens must study foreign languages for national security was not mistaken. One has to agree that our present conceptual way of coding and decoding (tying and untying) social and systematic codes of alien cultures is the cause of insecurity and tensions in the world today. A person, by the negative labels one sticks on other people, blinds and sinks oneself.

The African Book Without Title shows how strong and deep-rooted the concept of coding and decoding [kânga ye kutula makolo] was and still is throughout life in the African concepts. For those interested in the study of African thoughts and systems, we also recommend the reading of *Ku Nènga* and *Makuku Matatu*.

K. Kia Bunseki Fu-Kiau
J.P., Cambridge, 1980

A Few Words to the Second Edition

Twenty-one years ago this study was printed to serve as a stepping ground to my class discussions at Yale University. Since its publication, many outside of the classroom wanted to have a copy of *African Book Without Title*, but it was not available. Friends asked to review the materials and expand the book for a new edition. This was not possible because each time I tried to do so I continued to push the work off to the next day. Meanwhile demands and requests for the book accumulated. Finally, I decided to review the materials of the study for a second edition, which we are happy to present to you now under a new title *African Cosmology of the Bantu–Kongo: Principles of Life and Living.*

Is there any difference in form and content between this edition and the first? My answer to that question will be yes, indeed. Its content was revised and expanded where it was possible. This expansion includes a brief description of the Bântu-Kôngo concept of mapping the universe [kayèngele/luyalungunu] and a new chapter on the "Vee", one of the most secret aspects of the Bântu teaching among the Kôngo people.

By reviewing and expanding the old edition, we only had one desire in mind, to see many people walk into this new edition, not only with their fingers and eyes, but with both their minds and hearts and take it as one of the basic tools to understanding the "scientific" structures of the development of old, African traditional scholarship and its ancient schools.

African Cosmology of the Bantu–Kongo is not a collection of some data for some academic exercise which, usually, consists of transferring bones from one graveyard to another. It is a mound of raw materials that require sharp tools and trained minds to work with for individual, societal, and/or academic interests. One has to see it and accept it as a small, but not unimportant piece being added upon our universal, accumulative experience of knowing. Its completion was not simple. Behind its present form stands many close and distant collaborators of whom I will not hesitate to mention, some with all my gratitude: Danny Dawson who pushed so hard to see this book revised and expanded for a second edition. His advice and support were immeasurable. Franklin Stevenson, who skillfully illustrated this edition. Robert Marriott, Lisa Jones and Sarah Khan were essential to the editing process. And last but not least, Catheryn Vatuone, who volunteered not only to read, but edit and type the revised work, Anthony Ferreira and my publishers Roger and Rudolph Francis, Athelia Henrietta Press, Publishing in the Name of Orunmila.

Finally, my profound gratitude to all my masters, dead and alive, who knew how to open my eyes to this rich, traditional African "scholarship" that still flourishes in the wilderness of the minds of the African living libraries.

K. Kia Bunseki Fu-Kiau
Boston, June, 1998/2000

Tying the Spiritual Knot

African Cosmology of the Bântu–Kôngo

Principles of Life & Living

1

Kôngo Cosmology In Graphics

The following graphics about Kôngo concepts of their world are excerpts based on my book *N'kôngo ye nza yakun'zungidila/Le Mukôngo et le Monde qui L'Entourait* (ONRD, Kin 1969) and on my unpublished manuscripts *Ku Nènga: Verité Sur les Grandes Initiations en Afrique Centrale* (1973, pp. 300), and *Makuku Matatu: Les Fondements Culturels Kôngo* (1978, pp. 450). A summary understanding of these concepts, graphically, is of great help in order to comprehend the main ideas to be discussed in this work: *African Cosmology of the Kongo Bantu*. In this book I discuss certain concepts such as that of law and crime which link living communities to their ancestors, the spiritualized beings. For an African Mûntu, the dead are not dead: they are beings living just beyond the wall waiting for their probable return to the community [ku nseke], to the physical world.

A straight line/skyline [n'lônga - lukôngolo] or a line with an empty circle [mbûngi], in its middle is, among the Bântu-Kôngo, the symbol of emptiness, a world without visible life. That is the emptiness [mbûngi, mwâsi, mpâmpa]. The world in its beginning was empty; it was an mbûngi, an empty thing, a cavity, without visible life. There

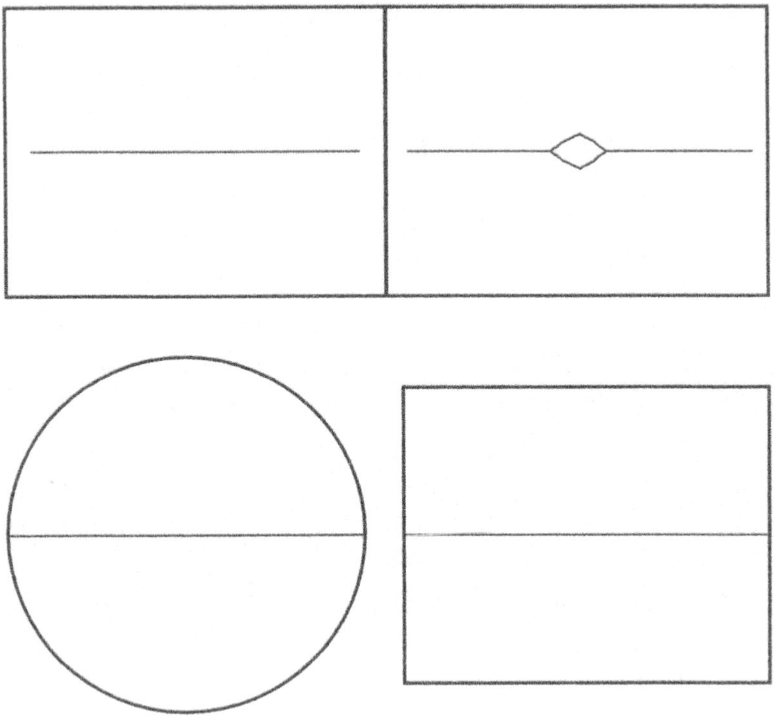

Figure 1.

are, in the empty mbôngi, active forces that can blow up [Mu mbûngi yampâmba mwena ngolo zilènda kubuka kadi zena môyo]. Where there is emptiness and nothingness, act other unknown forces, invisible of course [Kwena mwâsi ye mpâmba kweti sala ngolo zankaka zazîmbwa].

Man's life is surrounded by diverse forces and waves which govern it like in an mbungi [Luzîngu lwa mûntu i zîngu kia mbûngi kiazûngwa kwa ngolo ye minika mia mpila mu mpila miyâlanga kio].

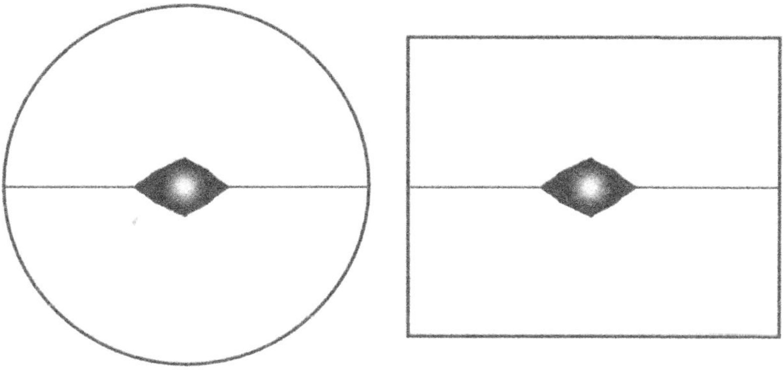

Figure 2.

A fire-force complete by itself, kalûnga, emerged within the mbûngi, the emptiness/nothingness and became the source of life [môyo wawo mu nza] on earth. That is, the kalûnga, complete force by itself, fired up the mbûngi and overran (dominated) it [kalûnga walûnga/kwîka mbûngi ye lungila yo].

The heated force of kalûnga blew up and down as a huge

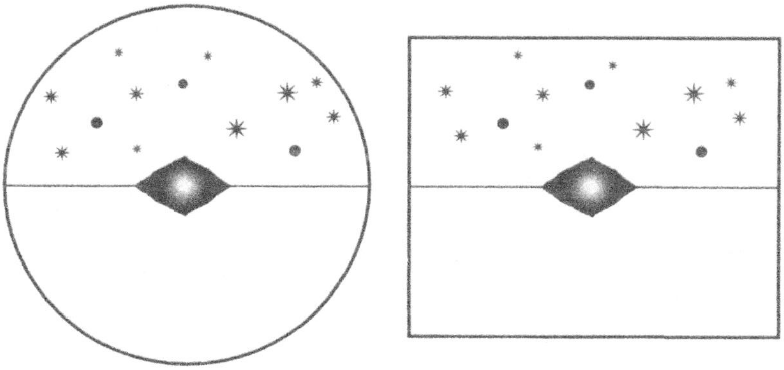

Figure 3.

storm of projectiles, kimbwandènde, producing a huge mass in fusion- [luku lwalâmba Nzâmbi] (Fu-Kiau, 1969). Kalûnga then became the symbol for force, vitality and more, a process and principle of change, all changes on the earth [Kalûnga walûnga mbûngi ye lungila yo wayika se n'kîngu wa nsobolo]. And by cooling the mass in fusion [zenge-zenge/ladi diambangazi] solidified itself [kînda] and gave birth to the earth. In the process of cooling, [mvodolo/nghodolo] the matter in fusion [luku lwalâmba Nzâmbi] produced water, [luku lwasânda] whose rivers, mountains, etc., are the results (Fu-Kiau, 1969).

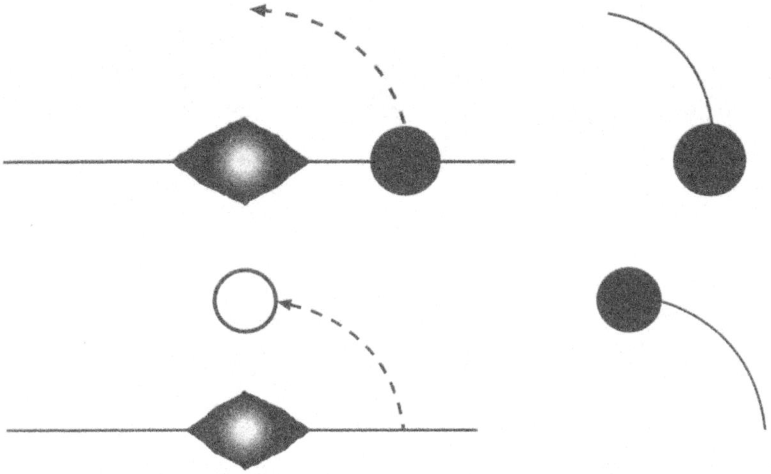

Figure 4.

The world, [nza], became a physical reality floating in kalûnga (in the endless water within the cosmic space); half emerging for terrestrial life and half submerging for submarine life and the spiritual world. The kalûnga, also meaning ocean, is a door and a wall between those two worlds. Kalûnga became also the idea of immensity, [sènsele/wayawa] that one cannot measure; an exit and entrance, source and origin of life, potentialities [n'kîngu-nzâmbi] the principle god-of-change, the force that continually generates. Because kalûnga was the complete life, everything in touch with the earth shared that life, and became life after itself. That life appeared on the earth under all kinds of sizes and forms: plants, insects, animals, rocks, human beings, etc. (see in Kindoki, 1970).

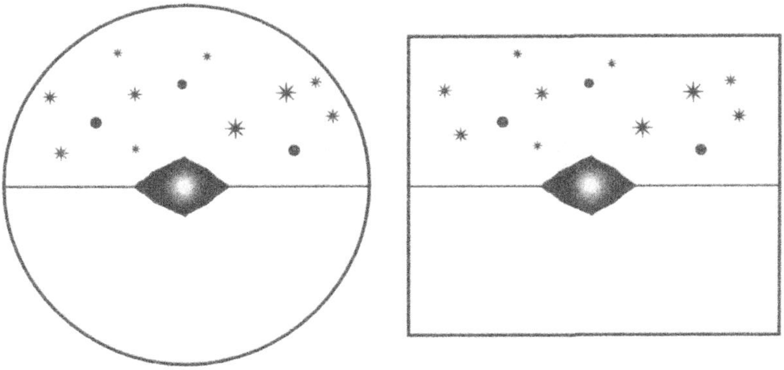

Figure 5.

The number of infinite mass in fusion particles that remained hanging in the upper space [mu luyalungunu] constituted what are known in human languages as sun, moon, stars [ntângu, ngônda, mbwetete] which are in realities other worlds. Man is called to live in certain of those worlds, too (Fu-Kiau, in Môyo, 1969). Kalûnga, the principle-god-of change, is a force in motion, and because of that our earth and everything in it is in perpetual motion. Man himself is an "object" [ma] in motion for he is an around-path-goer [n'zûngi a nzila], in his upper and lower world (Fu-Kiau, 1969). I would like to digress here to give you a brief Bântu-Kôngo concept of mapping the universe according to their teaching. An important step to help you understand more clearly some of the concepts described in this book.

Mapping the Universe

For the Bântu people, the Kôngo in particular, the universe as we see and know it is the result of the "primitive" event that occured *in* and *around* it [dûnga kiantete] well known as luku lwalâmba Nzâmbi, God cooked dough, i.e., the magmatic matters, the big bang (Fu-Kiau, 1969). It is the result of an expanding fire process that leaves behind, through a cooling process [nghodolo], satellites and planets. It is the process of the cosmic, expanding fires [dingo-dingo dia mpiâya yayalanga].

According to the Kôngo teaching, our planet earth was the starting point of this fire [mpiâya yâyi,center/didi] in our solar system [kûndu kièto, nza, i kènko dia ntônono a mpiâya yâyi mu fu kia ntângu]. On the ground of this old Bântu teaching, the universe can be mapped [tendumunwa/yalwa] in three main layers or zones [nyalu/zûnga], depending if it is in green, gray or red state.

a) **Green or breathing planet**
[nza yankûnzu/yavûmuna].

Green or breathing planets are living planets because they have completed the four great formation stages of the

Kôngo cosmogram known as dikenga dia Kôngo (Fu-Kiau, 1969, 1980, 1991). The key word to these planets is greenness [bunkûnzu], the vitality giving nature.

Green planets, like our own planet earth, can be thought of as the oldest planets to solar systems. The earth, for example, can be seen for the Bântu people as the oldest planet of the solar system. Green planets occupy the center [didi] of systems in our expanding universe.

The expanding creative fire-energy that departed from the first event [dûnga kiantete] or the big bang [kimbwandènde], was not an experimental explosion from a laboratory say the Bântu-Kôngo. It was a natural (call it divine) imperative order to bring a transformation process into being throughout the universe and into all its planets until their full maturity, i.e. be able to breathe and give/carry life [vûmuna ye vâna/tambikisa môyo]. To our present "knowledge", our planet, the earth, is the only planet known that has so far fulfilled this order: It is green (breathes) and does not only give life, but is able to sustain it up to now as well.

b) **Gray planets** [nza yavèmba].

Gray planets are planets "without" life yet. They are without life yet because these planets are still in their cooling [ghola] process stage, eventually heading towards their second, third, and fourth stage of dikenga dia Kôngo, Kôngo cosmogram's greatest stages as described by my works (1969, 1986, 1991). The moon [ngônda] and the planet mars [n'kasi a ngônda], which means "wife of the moon", are of this stage.

Planets in this group occupy the second layer of the map,

immediately after the green planets' layer. The key word in this zone [lubata] is grayness/dust [vèmba/fundu-fundu], but also dryness [yuma]. These planets are naked, dry and covered with dust. Gray planets are without life as we know it, i.e., they are without plants, animals, and of course, without human beings. The Bântu-Kôngo teaching suggests that if left alone, these planets will eventually complete the four stages of planet transformation process which is based on the Kôngo cosmogram, i.e., see the rise of plants, animals and beings like humans share life on them.

c) **Red/hot planets** [nza ya mbengelele].

Red or hot planets are actually burning planets. They are still matters in fusion without a clearly defined shape or form [zenge-zenge diatiya kôndwa mbèlo yasukuswa]. They are at their primitive or "first" stage of planetary formation process, their big bang stage [kimbwandènde]. These planets form the actual last frontier of a system, such as our own. Beyond these frontiers are infinite dark fields to be invaded by the future firing process [dingo-dingo] of expanding systems.

The key words in this zone [lubata] are extreme heat [mbengelele], and greatest temperature [mbangazi]. Here everything is matter in fusion and gas [zenge-zenge ye kaudi]. The red planets without form cannot avoid the dingo-dingo process of the four greatest stages of planetary transformation process of the dikenga, the cosmogram mentioned earlier. They will solidify through the cooling process, then eventually complete all other stages until the cosmogram [dikenga] of each planet is made whole to bear life. Until then, planets in this zone [lubata], because of the intensity of movements, will always continue to collide and shoot in the space [bulana ye tûmba mikala]. The following illustration shows the Bântu-Kôngo mapping concept of the universe [ngyalumun'a nkwal'a luyalungunu] Each circle represents the boundary between planets' zone layers.

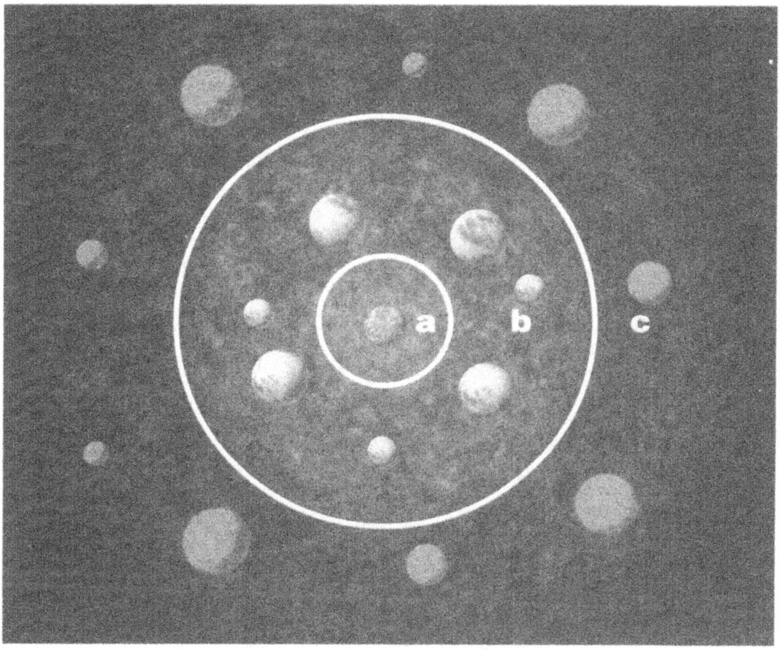

Figure 6.

After this short and brief description of the Bântu-Kôngo traditional scholarship on mapping the universe, let's return to the sun's apparent movements around our own planet and its impact or significance in the Kôngo system of thought.

Man is a second sun rising and setting around the earth.

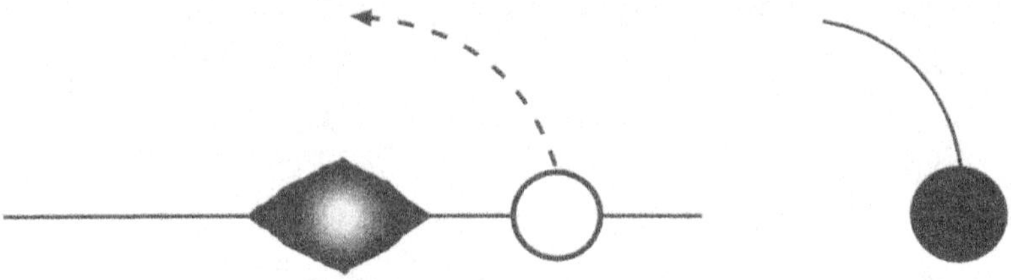

Figure 7.

He has to rise as the sun does in order to Kala, to be, to become, to light fire. The Kala and kalazima concept itself is associated with blackness and is used as a symbol of emergence of life, the physical world [ku nseke]. The ngûnza, spiritual man, is associated with the forces behind this concept and this process. Kala is the strongest will of mûntu's existence as we meet it in his daily expressions:

- Kala/ba mûntu—be a human being, a helpful being
- Kala/ba n'kisi a kânda—be the community's medicine
- Kala/ba nkasi a kânda—be a leader of the community
- Kala/ba ngânga—be a specialist, a true knower, a master, a doer
- Kala/ba n'kîngu a kânda—be the principle of the community
- Kala/ba kimpa mu bimpa—be a system within systems
- Kala/ba dièla mu bimpa bia mûntu—be wise and sensible to human systems
- Kala/ba kala, i sa vo n'zimi ye n'kwîki—be alive, be a (coal-fighter), i.e. extinguisher and lighter
- Kala/ba mfumu ye ngânga—be a leader and specialist

- Kala/ba lembanzau kia kânda—be the strongest of the community
- Kala/ba n'kôngo ye n'konguludi a kânda—be a Mukôngo and judge of his community

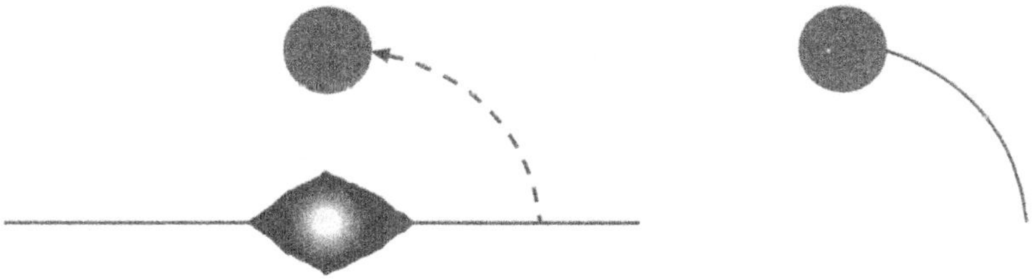

Figure 8.

Kula, to grow in the way of making one's own history [kikulu] to develop, to mature until reaching the position of leadership and be able to exercise it. Being in the king or leader's place is to be in the position of authority and power. The kala, by the process of growth and maturation, becomes tukula, the red or redness, which is the symbol of mature leadership within the community; it is also the step of the man of deeds [n'kwa-mâvanga]. The collective maturation, its leadership, through the process of collective growth, allows for social and community development. The step Kala-Tukula segment, representing the present time, is the positive one in the upper world, ku nseke, the physically living world.

The tukula position occupies the center of the cone of power and leadership [sudi kia lèndo], which I may also call the "V of life." To grow, to mature [kula] is to be ready to enter into this powerful zone of the V of life. It is very important to understand also that to enter the V of life zone is to stand vertically [telama lwîmba-ngânga]inside the V of life [V kia zîngu]. To stand vertically, like a master [ngânga] between the earth and the sky [va kati kwa n'toto ye zulu] and between the upper world and the lower world [va kati dia ku nseke ye ku mpèmbe].

The Egyptian ankh symbol itself is nothing else but a symbol of a master [ngânga] standing vertically inside the

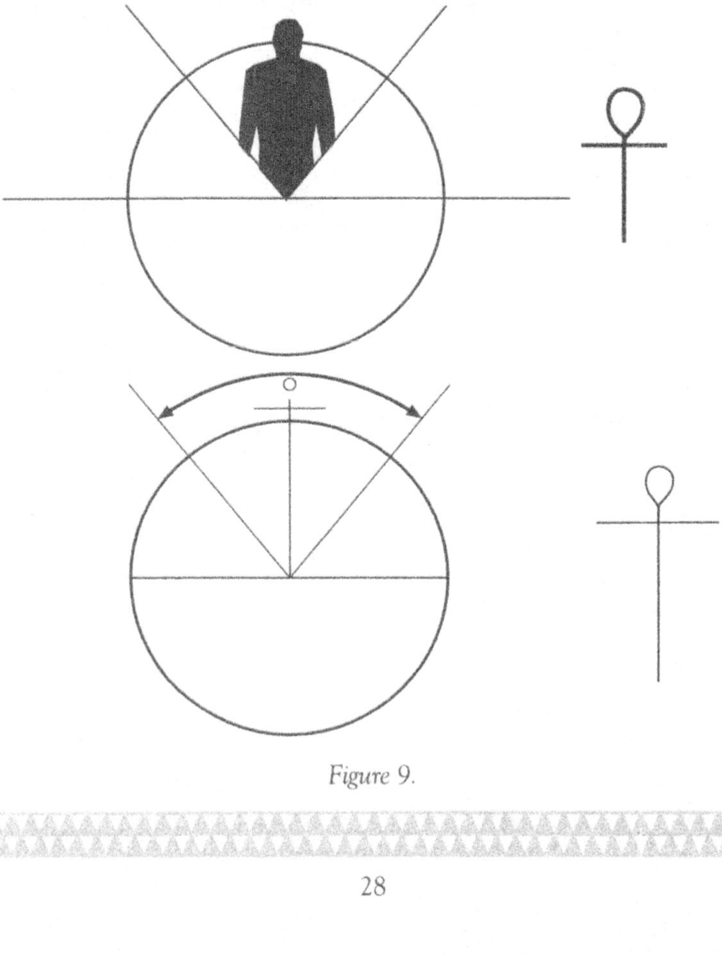

Figure 9.

"V" of his community life, as a priest and a leader. The fate of societies, institutions, and social systems all depend on how people of a given society enter this zone.

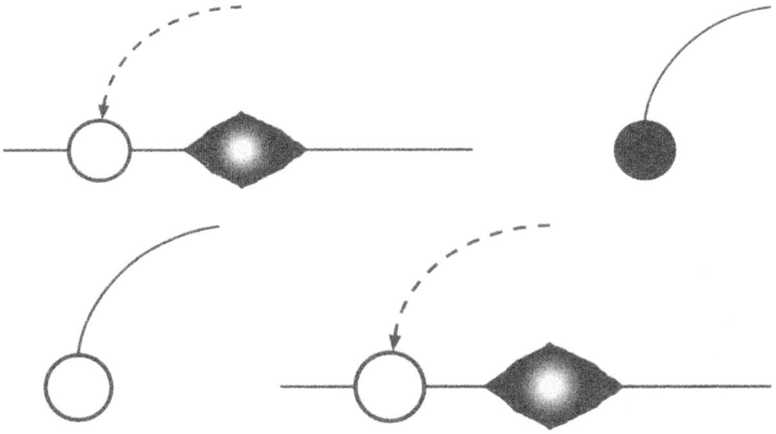

Figure 10.

Mûntu ukulanga uvânganga kikulu ye kota mu n'lônga wa Bakulu bateka kula. Mûntu wakuya kavânganga kikulu ko; ukotanga mu n'lônga wa bakuya, n'kuyu, i bakulu bambi.—A man that grows up is in the process of making history, and he enters the rank of the ancestors, those well minded people who grew up before him. On the contrary, a man that does not grow up, the one who deviates and is not well minded, is not in the process of making history; he enters the rank of the [n'kuyu] bad ancestors, while living, the deviators, the regressive and "stunted" ancestors.

These ancestors are those individuals who were not able to "telama lwîmba-nganga", to live inside their most aspired V of life zone, the V3. They passed this zone of power, creativity, inventions, and mastery in all aspects of life in a state of blindness. They were asleep, stunted ancestors [Bakulu bakuya].

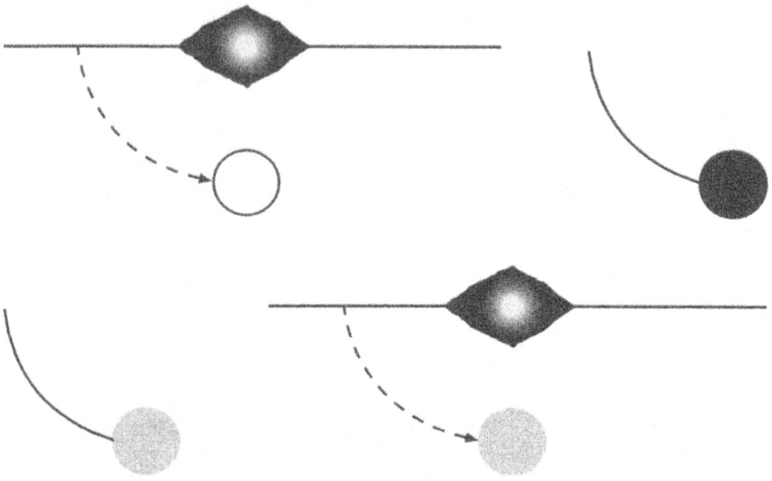

Figure 11.

Lândila tâmbi kia tukula, i bôbo bimvuka ye zinsi, mûntu fwiti kulumuka ku mpèmba. Nkulumukunu ku mpémba i kota mu n'soko wa nsobolo kana vo yakula evo yakuya—After his tukula step, man must descend into the deepest world. This is the same for communities, societies, and nations. The descent at ku mpèmba is to enter, positively or negatively, the process of change. Luvèmba, white chalk, is the symbol used at this step. Luvèmba also means negative elements (toxins) accumulated by a person during his life which leads to the physical death of all living beings. This process is associated with the ngânga, specialist or healer. The life/death struggle is experienced here. The step tukula-luvèmba in the upper world [ku nseke] is a negative one; it represents the future. This step is also the step symbolizing the process by which former leaders [sîmbi bia nsi] pass over their leadership to the younger generation, very often by initiation [ghândisa biyînga mu kubayekudila kingânga ye kimbuta]. It is the principle of receiving and releasing or the process of life and living [I n'kîngu wa tâmbula ye tambikisa evo dingo-dingo dia luzîngu] (Fu-Kiau, 1966).

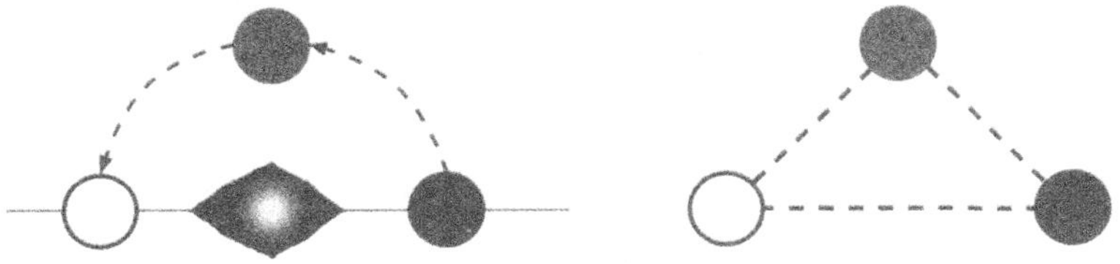

Figure 12.

This world, the physical world, has three basic forces whose leadership is the balance between them. This upperworld is widely known in Kôngo traditional symbolizing system as makuku matatu, three firestones, from the Kôngo well known proverbial theory—Makuku matatu matedimina kînzu kia Ne-Kôngo. The three firestones which uphold the social Kôngo structural motor, kînzu. The social structural organization of Kôngo society is shaped and patterned by three basic forces:

1. All growing social forces among zingûnza, heroic youth, future community members, in their kala step.
2. All positive capacities of present leaders and their leadership, n'twâdisi/sîmbi ye kintwâdisi kiâu.
3. The experience of specialists and their specialities, nkuma za bangânga ye kingânga kiâu.

Notice here, that in traditional Kôngo society, to become

a specialist, was something required of all its members, and was an expression of professional requirement in social life. In Kôngo society, "Everyone is a free individual and a doer/specialist," Muna Kôngo mfumu na mfumu, ngânga na ngânga. A Mukôngo was accepted as such, as an Ngânga in his community if he only could be a doer of something for the well-being of the community; kala ye salu, to have a "métier". This Nza ya ku nseke upper world is based in the real life:

> Sun movement: the rising and setting of the sun.
> Cycle of human life: birth, growth and death.
> Fireplace [zikwa], with its three firestones.
> Divinitory calabash in upper world with its three differently colored ingredents, dîngu.

According to the author Batshikama, also a Mukôngo, makuku matatu, the three Kôngo mother provinces which only date from the 13th century to the present time is not to be linked to the Bântu-Kôngo world view. Batshikama's concept of makuku matatu is incorrect. Makuku Matatu, which means the three firestones, is linked with the Kôngo worldview, through its presence in Kôngo cosmogram. The three firestones, or the physical world, [kala, tukula and luvèmba] are opposite of the spiritual world, Ku Mpèmba. This theory dates back to the beginning of the Kôngo language and culture. The concept of makuku matatu (machua among the Baluba) as a symbol of the upper world, is widespread among the Bântu populations, and yet, there too, it does not have any connection with the erroneous idea of the Batshikama notion stated in his "Voici les Jagaz" (p. 179). The Kôngo ignore Batshikama's theory of makuku matatu because it presents the notion of recent, pre-colonial three mother provinces without connecting their basic and symbolic meaning with the social structural forces of the three firestones.

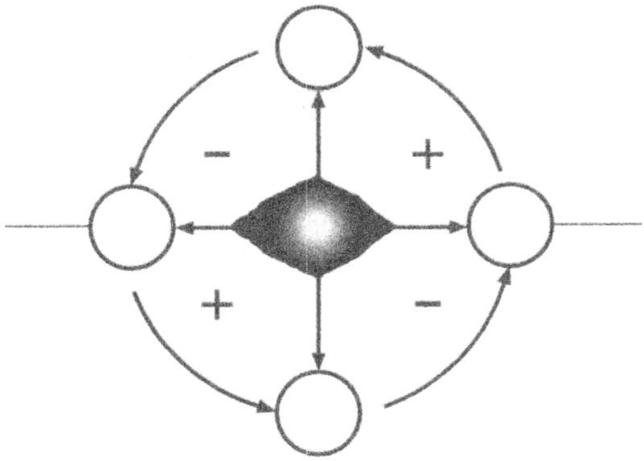

Figure 13.

After crossing the kalûnga line, the doorway towards ku mpêmba, the lowest world, the dead, i.e., the transformed body, grows up too in order to reach the position of musoni, (of sona, i.e., to mark on, to symbol, to engrave) and become a true knower of what is marked on one's own mind and body.

The position of musoni is associated with the notion of ndoki, the knower of man's principles and systems of n'kîngu ye bimpa higher levels, the kindoki or science of higher knowledge. The manipulation of these n'kîngu and bimpa principles and systems permitted, say the Kôngo, to assist the ndoki to become a winged person, a flier. An ndoki was publicly affirmed to have "flown from here to

Kinkènge and from there to Boma" during a public confession (Diantèzilza, 1970).

Musoni represents the color yellow, which is believed to be associated with knowledge. In an initiatic ceremony leading to the deepest things, an initiator ngânga will begin his rite by saying Ntete mpèmba mbo' musoni kalânda. In the ceremony of the descent of passage, first comes luvèmba, then musoni, the yellow, which reminds the ngânga that things should be done in their natural order. One does not go beyond this deepest world, ku mpèmba without passing through luvèmba, the death barrier, the doorway towards it.

The step luvèmba-musoni at ku mpèmba is a positive one; it is the period of birth-growth of that world, a penetration through the accumulated cultural roll of the past time in order to regenerate one's own life's potentialities for a possible return of that ngolo, energy, ku nseke, in the physical world.

After accumulation of all spiritual, moral, intellectual or genetic potentialities at ku mpèmba, when passing through

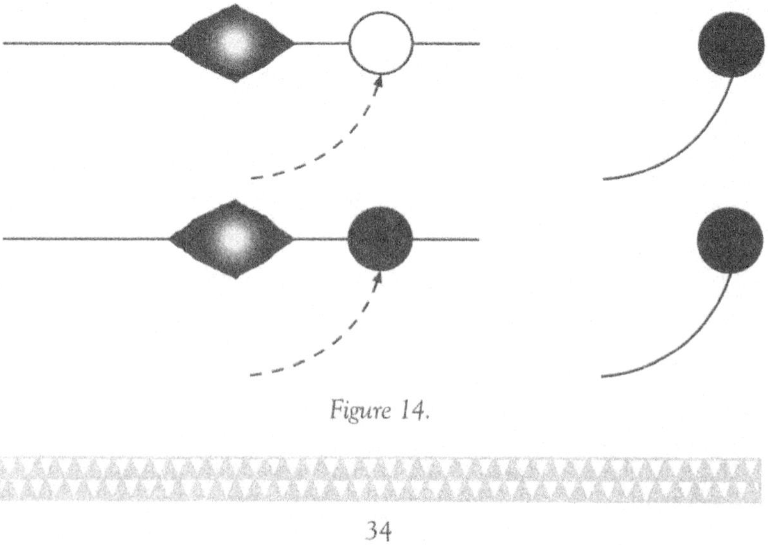

Figure 14.

the step of musoni, the Kôngo cosmology tells us, the dual soul-mind mpève-ngîndu is ready to reincarnate (rebirth or re-re . . . birth) in order to rise again in the upper world [kala diâka ku nseke]. This is demonstrated in a continuum of rebirth after rebirth, meaning incarnation after incarnation. The body of ku mpèmba has then to change (die) in order to be acceptable by an upper world's physical body. The step musoni-kala in the spiritual world is a negative one because it represents the departing step of all descending forces/energies of the lower world.

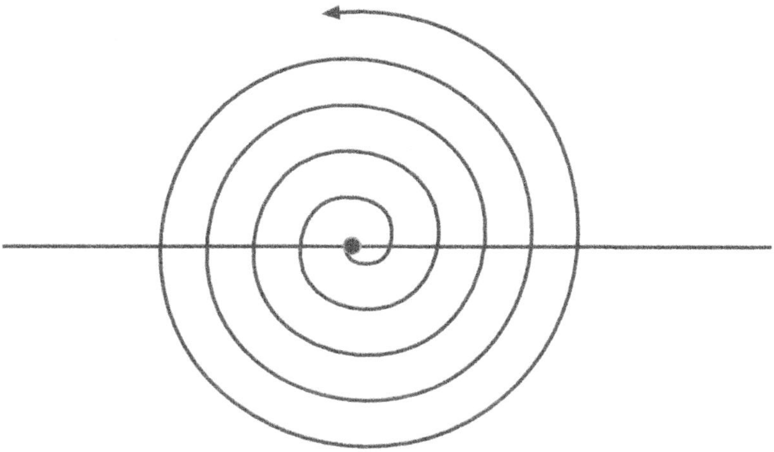

Figure 15.

A human being's life is a continuous process of transformation, a going around and around, Mûntu ye zîngu kiândi i madièdie ye n'zûngi a nzila. The human being is kala-zima-kala, a living-dying-living-being. A being of continuous motion through four stages of balance between a vertical force and a horizontal force. The horizontal force is fundamental, because it is the key to open or to close, to enter or exit the diurnal world, nza a mwîni, ya ku nseke or the nocturnal world, nza ya mpîmpa, ya ku mpèmba and vice versa. The vertical force, the dangerous and dominant one, is secondary in the balance required for community life [kinenga kia kimvuka], its religious relations.

It is the horizontality plane [lufulu lwabwa/lufulu lwa kilukôngolo] that binds all community relationships between its members: its true religion [lukangudulu]. When these relationships are weakened or broken, the community leadership calls for a reconciliation meeting [mu kangulula] to tie again, to *re-ligar*; the broken relationships are reestablished and the community is balanced [kinenga]. Once these broken relationships are reestablished and the community bio-spiritual "rope" is strengthened, the whole community will stand again lwîmba-ngânga on the vertical plane [kintombayulu] between the earth and the skies, and between the upper and lower world, to communicate to both kalûnga, the completely complete higher living energy [Nzâmbi], and the ancestors [Bakulu].

The Kôngo believe that individual people and nations have rolls of life [tuzîngu] in the form of tapes that hold (imprint) records of all their deeds. Because of these rolls hidden in their beings, their past can be revealed, i.e., read like a book [zingumunwa]. On the day of "judgment", the sacred teaching of the Kôngo philosophy- says that each will see his roll of life [luzîngu] unfold and speak loudly before the universe and its "great judge."

Figure 16.

Man's life attention, ku nseke, is centered on the n'kisi (N) which is the central and most important element in that world. It is the force-element that has the power to "kînsa", root-word of n'kisi, meaning to take care, to cure, to heal, to guide by all means even by ceremony. The n'kisi takes care of human beings in all his aspects of life in the world because he has a material body that needs care by n'kisi (medicine). Because he lives in a world surrounded by matadi (M), minerals, bimbenina (B), plants, and bulu (b), animals, his n'kisi (N) must be made of compounds from M-B-b.

In the spiritual world the kundu, kindoki, is the central and most important element in this unfathomable world. This element is made up by the experience based on bibulu (b) including human being, the sîmbi (s) i.e., ancestral experience, and on mpève(m), i.e., soul-mind experience. In this case kundu or kindoki is the lived and accumulated knowledge. This lived accumulated experience-knowledge may be positive or negative for the social life in the community depending on the kind of leadership it has. Because of its double faces, one positive and another negative, it became kundu-man is a liar [kundu n'kwa-mikalu]. One cannot tell about himself what he is, says a Kôngo proverb.—Kundu is alike to properties; no one agrees to be rich [Kundu kimvwâma, ka kitambudulwanga ko]. The fact of not agreeing to one's own wealth does not mean that wealth is totally bad. Kindoki, nzailu likewise, is one among the equivalent terms of science in kikôngo language, and as to every knowledge it has its positive side as well as its negative one. Kindoki, Nzailu and Bumpitu are synonymous terms, but the last is more proper in lieu of chemistry than in lieu of science.

Nothing in the daily life of Kôngo society is outside of

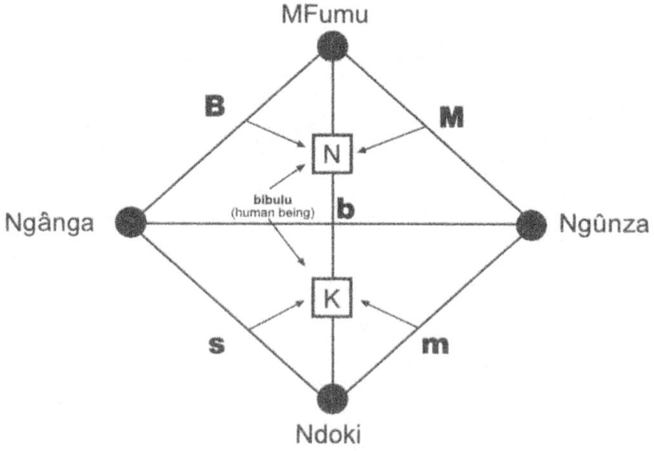

Figure 17.

its cosmological practices. The marriage pattern itself, one of the most important social institutions, symbolizes a basic cosmological pattern where vertical and horizontal forces are keys to that most important institution. Notice the position of each element allied to marriage lôngo. Lôngo itself occupies the position of center (didi), the source of radiation of life. The marriage, in other words, for the Bântu-Kôngo, is a physically living symbol of alliance(s) between, at least, two communities. Therefore, divorce is not an issue of individuals, but of communities involved in the marriage. There is no such thing as "love" in the beginning of a marriage. Love is a process of mutual growth of partners-symbols of communities' alliances. For the Bakôngo, no matter what happens among partners in the lôngo, that lôngo will be held alive as long as alliances between the communities involved remains on good

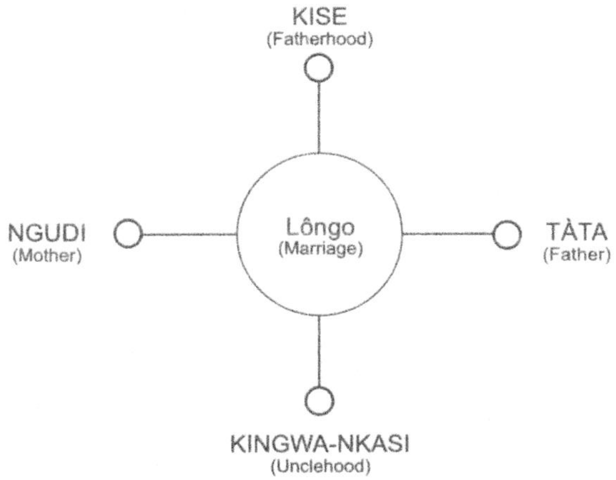

Figure 17b.

terms. These communities will do their best in order to maintain alive the lôngo.

The marriage, first of all, is a social "deal" for the great interest of the community and its members. It is through family buta, that social forces are transmitted such as norms, values, ideals, etc. Without accord of those forces, it is almost impossible among the Kôngo that individuals legally, according to the traditions, form a family buta, no matter how much they love each other. A "buta" formed outside of that accord is always seen socially as "illegal", a social deviation to the part of partners, for lôngo is more than the union of two individuals. Since the children to be born/ engendered by the partners in their lôngo should serve the community, it is important that, that same community or communities have a word to say at the moment the will of lôngo formation appears, i.e., it should be prepared to accept them in recognizing first of all the union of the parents, and this, publicly within the communities, otherwise they will give birth to children, which will, because of social and psychological crisis they may have, become bad leaders or dictators as revenge against the society.

Moreover, all social forces watch at lôngo, the indissoluble institution (in Kôngo tradition, there is no legal aspect of lôngo-divorce). Lôngo creates alliances and neutralizes conflicts among parties. The child does not belong to parents, it is a collective, and societal relationship, says a proverb [Wabuta mbâwu ândi kayetila]. By recognizing the lôngo as legal, the society accepts automatically the responsibility to raise all offspring's of such a "lôngo"

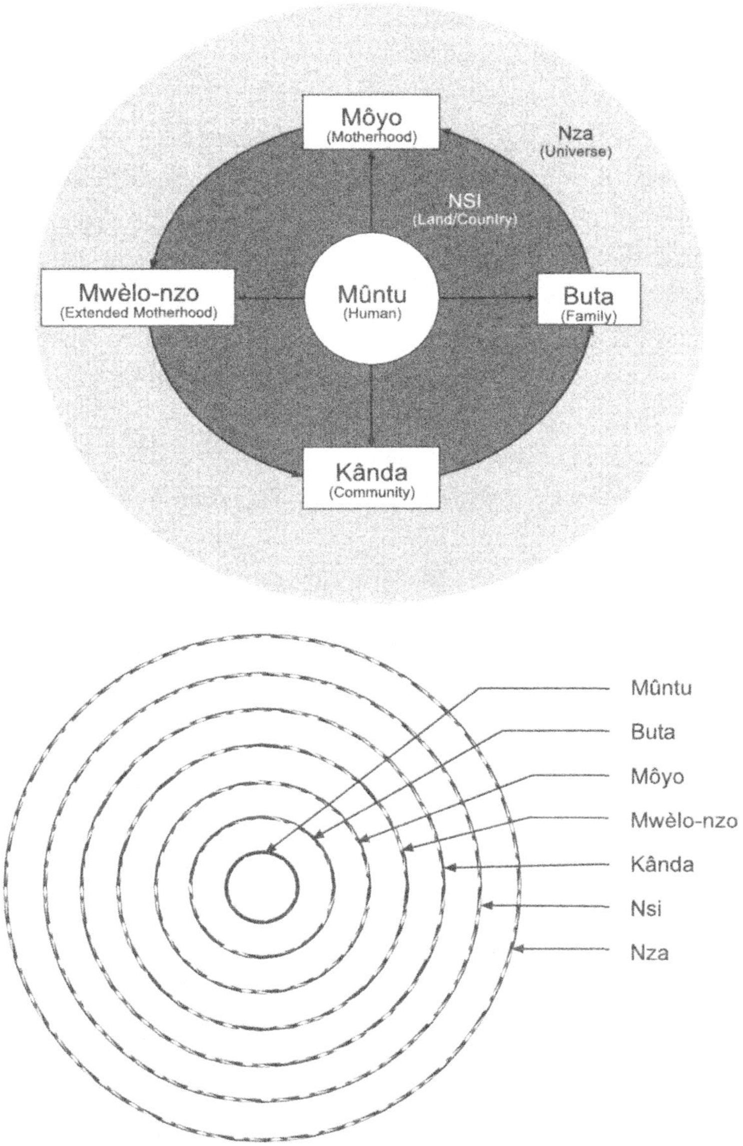
Môyo
(Motherhood)
Nza
(Universe)
NSI
(Land/Country)
Mwèlo-nzo
(Extended Motherhood)
Mûntu
(Human)
Buta
(Family)
Kânda
(Community)
Mûntu
Buta
Môyo
Mwèlo-nzo
Kânda
Nsi
Nza

Figure 18.

whereby the African saying, "It takes the whole community/village to raise a child."

N'kângi-dikânda, the clan's pattern, is a structured totality of structured totalities within a great ensemble of ensembles.

Mûntu, person: set of concrete social relationships, he is a system of systems, the pattern of patterns in being.

Buta, family: father and mother with or without children of their own. In Black African society a man/woman without child has always, in accordance to kinship relationship, those to whom he/she is father/mother with all respect due to a father/mother throughout all social layers from the buta to the nza itself.

Môyo literally, womb: set of family members of one's grandmother's descent.

Mwèlo-nzo: set of miôyo (plural of môyo)

Kânda: community, set of mièlo-nzo (plural of mwèlo-nzo); an ethnic group or a bio-branch with its own "praise name", ndumbudulu.

Nsi (n'toto): land, region, country

Nza: world, universe.

This last concept, the clan's pattern, and all others shortly described above are among those expressing the Kôngo concept of the world, the Kôngo cosmology. Without this brief summary, I thought it would be difficult for certain readers to comprehend the African concept of law and crime which will now be discussed below. Many conceptual parts of that African traditional legal aspect will be easily understood thanks to some of the previous explanations. I, now, invite you to read that African aspect of law and crime even though it is not done by a specialist in legal matters.

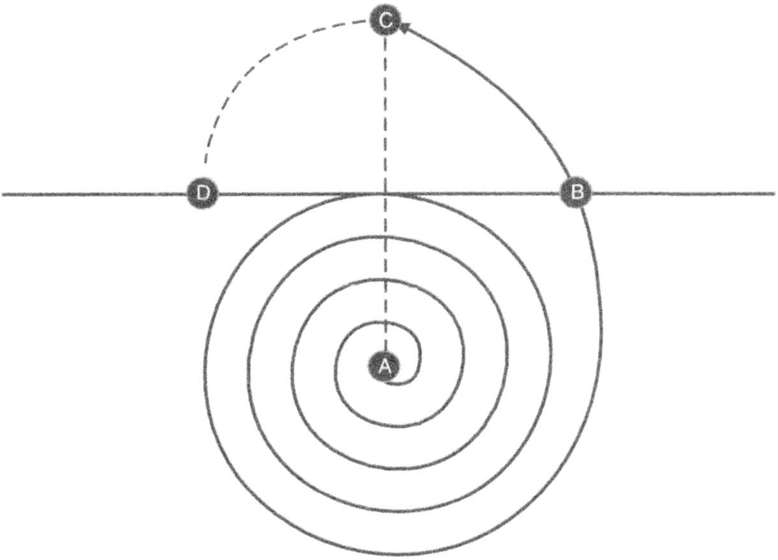

Figure 19.

A - Nkata ku mfînda i ntângu a bakulu ye sîmbi - The spiral bale (coil) in the forest (spiritual world) represents the past, i.e., ancestors and genius' time [Ntângu yankulu/tându kiankulu (A)].

B - The sun rising segment (BC) represents the present time whose the "n't-inu" (sîmbi) is "n'kam'a ntângu", the dam of time.

C - The sun setting segment (CD) represents the future, i.e. the time after the king (n'tinu) or a djin (sîmbi) and his leadership. A forecast of what one will be, an "n'kulu" (ancestor) or an "n'kuyu"(ghost, bad ancestor,), on the eyes of the society once one is gone "ku mpèmba" (died).

2

AFRICAN CONCEPT OF LAW AND CRIME

This study on the African concept of law and crime is based on the Bântu people who live in the center of west Africa, specifically the Bântu-Kôngo. In this analysis I would like to emphasize the traditional concepts of law and crime still practiced by the Bântu-Kôngo people and their neighbors rather than what has been recorded by some European travelers. These Europeans wrote about the culture of the people of this area, including the Bântu-Kôngo, without knowing, even superficially, any African language, man's most important instrument of cultural communication and of social learning patterns and behavior.

One of the most crucial African problems, which leads to anarchy within many African governments today, and therefore cannot be neglected, is the African people's total ignorance of their own traditional concept of law and crime. This ignorance confronts modern African leaders with a dilemma, a certain impossibility of choice. Because they do not have a full understanding of either western or African patterns of law, they cannot totally opt for either system.

With the adoption of the imported legal systems by new African nations, everything since then has turned upside down. Considering what one sees and lives in today's Africa, colonial atrocities are not any more viewed as such. For many outsiders who have witnessed African humanism and its strong wonderful neighborhood among people, verbally and documentary these outsiders tell us that Africa, in many of its parts, is in the wrong hands of "foolish" leaders. African leaders, with few exceptions, are considered foolish men [bimpûmbulu, lauki ye m'bundumuni mia nsi], because they act outside of African traditional legal aspects of leadership. African people themselves agree that the great majority of their political leaders are good for nothing.These leaders could have been excellent governors during the colonial epoch to serve their masters sufficiently. But, by and large, we should recognize one competence: They are very successful about the matter of the competition around colleagues' ladies, a competition that gave birth to what is known in certain African countries as "second-bureauism,"[1] the key to most antagonism in today's Africa; antagonisms which are not very often political or ideological.

---

[1] Second-bureauism: secret polygamy of elites and bourgeois in certain African countries. A second-bureau is, in those countries, not a second office, but a lady very often officially hired by a governmental or an administrative authority not essentially to play a governmental role in public life, but in the eyes of the hiring side, to serve as a means by which the authority intends to accomplish certain of its secret plans and intentions against certain individuals it considers as its foes.

Unfortunately, African people do not want to try to see through African legal and conceptual framework what is happening now to African leaders. There should be, they say, something wrong going on here. Well, a Kôngo philosophical principle and its variants will enlighten us on the issue. In considering the physical and mental health of a leader, the true leader for a people, the Kôngo people say: Community-chief/leader does not get mental disease [Mfumu-dikânda kalaukanga ko], except otherwise, according to the three variants of the precited principle on the health of a leader:

> Variant No 1: "Mfumu-dikânda kalauka milongi katundidi"—a societal leader becomes foolish if he bypasses his people's advice.
>
> Variant No 2: "Mfumu-dikânda kalauka bilesi katundidi"—a community leader becomes foolish if he usurps his people's prerogatives.
>
> Variant No 3: "Mfumu-dikânda kalauka yèmba katûmbudi"—a community leader becomes mentally sick if he intends to destroy the public's fundamental institutions, such as yèmba.

The Kôngo principle of political philosophy cited here tells us that a leader does not suffer any ailment due to his functions be it physical or mental during his mandate if he shares his power, his authority with the people through their elected delegates. On the contrary, according to these three variants of the principle, if he considers himself the law, the people, the synonym of institution, and the state then he may become the object of all kinds of troubles: Overworking or brain-fag, incapacity, nervousness, uncontrolled desire to stay in power, even if unable. Instead of being a leader who listens to the people, he becomes a leader that speaks, matokula, i.e., a leader that imposes on the people his own will contrary to the African traditional concept of a leader's conduct in public affairs. The leader has ears, he does not have a mouth ["Mfumu matu; kavwa n'nwa ko"]. Many African leaders, as well as intellectuals, continue to underestimate their own people by the single fact that those populations do not speak western languages, the "languages of science" as they say. For them, says the imperialistic anthropology of some fifteen years ago, those populations still have "archaic mentalities". That is a grave accusation.[2] For many leaders, African languages are the poorest ones in the world. They cannot, by any proof, accept that certain among our languages are by far richer than the languages of today's leading technology. With the English word COME "framed" by diverse prepositions, the Kongolese (Kikôngo) demonstrates the richness of African languages, languages considered by many as unable to transmit knowledge:

Come	Kwîza, lwâka, pala, vaikisa, lumina
Come (down)	Kulumuka, kôka
Come (out)	Vaika; lènda

---

2. See Th. Obenga in his *La Cuvette Congolaise*, pg. 73.

Come (in)	Kota, fiolumuka
Come (up)	Tômbuka, maka: sônga
Come (on)	Vova, tatamana; bwè kwândi
Come (back)	Vutuka; vutukila
Come (about)	Lwâka; zûngana, bwa
Come (across)	Bwâna; sabuka, luta
Come (along)	Nûnga; tatamana, bûndana, wîzana, zolana
Come (after)	Lânda, vîngana
Come (around)	Sîngisa, tambudila, siâmisa
Come (at)	Lwâka, tûla; bwîla
Come (between)	Vâmbisa, pwaka, zènga, kambakana
Come (out with)	Zâyisa, tèngula, samuna
Come (against)	Bulana, ta sâkuba, kondama, bûtana
Come (apart)	Mwângana, kukivâmbula, tatuka, tîna
Come (away)	Nânguka, lônduka
Come (before)	Tèkila, twâma, vita
Come (by)	Viôkila, lutila, yôkila
Come (over)	Bwîla, tâna, kwîza
Come (together)	Kutakana, yônzama, tôtana, bûndana
Come (under)	Tambudila, yâlwa

I sometimes ask myself for whom African, even the world's intellectuals and scholars do make fun of? I grew up in a village of at least 1,000 inhabitants (before it knew the rural exodus). There was not a single policeman, the jail was unknown, no secret agent, i.e., a people's watchdog. It did not have a bureau of investigation, no sentry to watch on people's goods. In daytime that village was practically and in its entirety empty without a single person to take care of unlocked doors. Strangers were always welcome. Everybody felt responsible to everybody else in the community and its neighborhood. When a community member suffered, it was the community as a whole that suffered. Until age 25, it was very nice to live in that community, literally a community without problems. Such communities still exist in many parts of the world which are known as "developing regions" where the imperialistic arms race did not yet trouble the peace. But take any modern African city (center of imported civilization) where we find thousands of policemen, security services, schools with their many hundreds of "civilizing" teachers, all kinds of counsellors, all kinds of knowledge unknown in rural milieus, and do not talk about warranted jobs! Could you imagine or tell how many corruptions, fights, insults, falsifications, discriminations, kidnappings, and crimes are made every single day by our leaders and intellectuals in such cities? Any of those cities are as alike as any city in the world. And my question remains, where is that Kimûntu (the state of being human), that we should be?

Africa is suffering now because it has chosen and adopted a law that has less to do with humanity, a law that emphasizes more the life of the disliked, undemocratic, and unpopular leaders and for the no-soul-minded-objects. The weight is so great upon African leaders' shoulders that it is impossible for them to think coherently, and consciously about their national responsibilities. Africa, under such a leadership with such a law, will be good for nothing. Our world needs a new order. Such an order is only possible with a new law in newly born countries. A law that should neutralize present world antagonisms. Africa may greatly contribute in building such an order if it chooses a law that sees man's value and needs first rather than his destruction. African people should unite and strongly stand on their own feet at this time where even the most democratic countries become undemocratic; a time where peace-keeping countries become dictator supporter countries; a time where human rights observers become human slaughter encouragers. African salvation will not come either from the East or from the West; it is entirely an African affair. Our world is frightened about anything because we are entirely dumped in an ocean of human blood and no one can breathe. I hope this study, in its perspective of traditional African law and crime, will be of interest to lawmakers and improve their understanding of these African concepts, especially those related to land and to social structure.

The study is not itself a comparative study of western and African concepts of law and crime, but a description of traditional African legal concepts among the Kôngo, one of the most important zones of the African culture. The elements of law described here could, in the future, serve as sources of information for a comparative study of law and crime. These concepts are important because they reflect the larger society and cultural history. Because of its alliance with western imperialist-capitalist masters, the present African leadership is developing legal systems on western grounds which lack a clear understanding of African cultural traditions in terms of law; traditions which should give rise to authentic and original African constitutions [tusikudukusu, pl. of Lusikudukusu].

It is almost impossible these days to avoid western even eastern influence on African legislature. But the tendency towards westernization or easternization of African legislature raises serious questions: Will western or eastern institutions imported into Africa fit into the cultural "tribal/ethnic" bases? Will not these bases be in perpetual conflict? Will not the replacement of traditional African laws based on taboo by western or other based laws cause some kind of social imbalance on African fundamental concepts and values? Is not the traditional taboo, collectivist or communalist African system the best system for African development? These are some important questions I would like to discuss, not as a specialist in the matter, but as an African who has been nourished by the daily life experience of this systematic African way of living for more than forty years in my African Kôngo community. Not in cities, but in the countryside where the real African life is met, and where most critical African problems are lived, and above all, where languages and cosmologies that generate all African thought and philosophy are still alive.

Most of today's African leaders, in their daily demagogic political speeches recognize that their countries do suffer from one mortal disease whose cure must be immediate. A disease that has become a keyword in all political, economic and philosophical debates in all societal levels worldwide: the question of exploitation. But what is very strange and imperceptible to any human mind is that these same leaders ignore the fact that they are, at the moment, the key-leaders of those African countries where exploitation persists at a faster rate than what was known during the colonial epoch. This exploitation has reached the highest point of national ruin. No one cares about real social and community needs; no one cares about what will be the national next day; no one cares about our positive old ways of thinking and of taking care of our fellow human beings; no one cares about our norms and values; no one cares . . . and so on and so forth, except planning who may be able to shoot at Kele-Kele-dia-Nsi, my opponent; digging for causes and reasons to eliminate anyone attacking insane political behaviors. What means are necessary to stop a particular region or ethnic group progressing in this country. That is the way of thinking and of acting, not of all African ordinary people, but of most of today's leaders of Africa; leaders that do nothing more than killing, hanging, corrupting and increasing the illness among us: the exploitation. It is certain that everybody agrees that as long as this disease remains in its present form, all of Africa will continue following the path of underdevelopment, i.e., of economic slavery. Its populations, the African people, be they Black or White, will remain ill-fed, ill-housed, ill-educated, ill-clothed, and perpetually victims of outside systems, ideologies, values and laws.

No, Africa needs a change because its' populations need it and not because someone else wants it for them. It belongs, first, to every African leader to have the deepest understanding of all of our regional cultures that symbolize ourselves if we hope for a true, real, and profound change in Africa, the first continent of mankind.

An African leader who considers as tribalism our national diversities commits a national crime because, by doing so, he himself denies the existence of the nation itself. Are not ethnic diversities that made USA, Russia and China, great nations! Ethnicity is not a disease, it is, in its diversity, a national pride. Nations are forests—"Nsi mfînda" says a Kôngo proverb. A forest of one type of trees is not a forest, it is a "n'dima" (orchard) no matter how large it is, for a forest is always an ensemble in diversity. Our national cultural, linguistic, artistic, and economic diversities are also our national pride on which our national African Constitutions should be based. These ideas are discussed, especially those based on Kôngo culture, a Bântu ethnic group in the center of west Africa. Let's now briefly talk about this cultural zone and its historical background.

III

Historical Background of the Kôngo Cultural Zone

Certain parts of Ex-Belgian Africa, as well as certain others of the Angolan Popular Republic and that of the Congo Popular Republic were constitutional parts of the Ancient Kingdom of the Kôngo that was destroyed by the Portugese and its allies in 1482. The Berlin Geographical Conference in 1884–85 divided this Kingdom into three imperialistic zones: One part, part of the present Angola, went to the Lusitanian imperio-dictatorial system; the second, part of the present Congo, to the imperialistic system of France, and the third, part of the present, undemocratic Democratic Republic of Congo, was made the private property of Leopold II, the King of Belgium.

Unable to develop his private property, this rich territory within what the colonists called the "dark continent" (a point of view that opposes that of the ancient Greeks who knew that Africa was the source of their scientific progress). Leopold II gave up the Congo at the consent of the Belgian people in 1908. The Congo of Leopold II then became the Belgian Congo. Since then the Congo entered a period during which its important traditional institutions were systematically destroyed. Boko, the most popular and most important school was destroyed; social and political institutions were prohibited. Kânda, the structural base of the African community life as well as its organizational patterns were disorganized. "Those who were people became apes," says a popular folk song which shows how colonial tortures transformed African people. We were people, but by exploitation we are made apes, working in corvee [Twabèdi kwèto bântu twayikidi bankewa; salanga! o kiniemo!].

The word Salongo, in lingala, is a deformation of kikôngo, "salanga", which had in that case negative connotations during the colonial epoch. It signified dictatorship, wicked authority, forced work, exploitation, and many other similar meanings. Today, it is a political motto, pure and empty pretension of certain African governments used to lead their countries if not to the first, to the second or to the third position of economic development, but never to the fourth one.

African authorities, because of their lack of collaboration with their well informed countrymen and scholars, tend to reverse the national historical truth. This is the case of Salongo in Mobutu's "Zaire", and many other cases. Salongo was a popular folk song among civilians as well as among militarymen. This folk song was the strongest popular song criticizing and insulting the Belgian colonial authority in Congo. This song is a veritable monument of attack against colonialism, the leopoldian one in particular, in central Africa during the time of what is known as "Effort de Guerre" (war effort). I produce here the lingala version of the song after corporal Bandi-Makaya, a veteran of

WWI(1914–1918), one of our best informants about our national oral history collected by our efforts at Luyalungunu lwa Kûmba-nsi Institute.

Salongo
E e e
Salongo
Alinga mosala
Biso tokoma bakoko na bino
Kosalela bino
Mosala ya mbongo
Lokola ebende (machine)

Salongo
E-e-e
Salongo
Alinga mosala
Biso tokuma baumbu na bino
Kotekisa biso
Na Saki ya mungwa
Lokola mosolo

Salongo
E e e, etc.
Biso tokoma banyama na bino
Kokengela bino
Na porte ya ndako
Lokola bapaya

Salongo
Biso tokoma bangamba na bino
Komemaka bino

(Na) Mapeka na biso
Lukula ba mpunda

Mondele mobomaka biso
Lokola ba niama zamba
Likolo mabele
Bakoko batikila biso
Salongo

Opposition against colonialism and exploitation led the country to fight for and win its freedom in 1960. The people's main goal at that time was to build the country upon traditional positive cultural values of all our regions' particularities. Values deeply rooted in our social organizations, in our traditional unwritten legislatures, the fu-kia-nsi, the national socio-structural systems.

Social Organization

The Kôngo society, as well as most African societies were and still are, communalistic, i.e., each community self-determines the social, political, economic organization and leadership. "The Kôngo had a king up until the time of colonization, but his position was decidedly titular" and the same author continues "The mode of production established a minimum dependence between different community segments and there was no private ownership of the means of production." (Kajsa, 1972:3)

Each local community or Vata, which is relatively independant, has two or more Belo. Each belo has two or more

Mièlo-nzo (sing Mwèlo-nzo/mwèlonzo). The Mwèlonzo is divided into Miôyo (singular Môyo). The Môyo is also termed as Buta. The Buta is the smallest but most important institution in Kôngo social and organizational structure. It is here that basic family education is carried out: language, parenthood relationships, a general knowledge concerning local plants as an introduction to popular medicine, community or ethnic history (law, migrations, ancestors), etc. Each of these divisions is a social and political entity which meets to discuss or to regulate community problems under the leadership of the wisest and strongest of the group.

The most important and powerful institution within the community, vata, is the Belo. The Belo is symbolized by its public house where social, political, economic and organizational issues are discussed before being discussed by the community assembly. This public house is called Boko [mbôngi, yèmba, lusânga, kiôto], a word that literally means "house without rooms", i.e., a house in which privacy has no room. I give here certain proverbs related to that basically very important Kôngo social institution, the BOKO:

1) "Boko wabokudisa nkuni mu vata." It is the boko that orders the collection of firewood in the village (to make a fire circle for a public hearing).

2) "Vata dikôndo mbôngi diafwa." A village without a boko is dead. A society without institutions where public freedom is warranted is straight to its fall.

3) "Boko wabokula mâmbu." It is the boko that breaks (cuts) the affairs in the community. All decisions in the community are public agreements made in public at ku boko, the public house.

4) "Boko wabôka mu vata . . ." It is the boko that calls for meetings in the village. Boko, the entire community, decries a state of emergency in the community.

5) "Mbila boko ni bèto kulu," the call of boko belongs to all of us. Public institutions are public; individuals cannot make them private affairs. The public call makes us all stand.

6) "Mbôngi wabônga mâmbu," variant "Mbôngi wabôkila mâmbu." It is the mbôngi that takes care, investigates, all affairs in the political, economic, social, and diplomatic matters, in order to discuss them publicly in the view and the hearing of all community members. Community alone can do what is best for its members.

7) "Lusânga wasangumuna mâmbu." It is the boko that raises problems and issues of all orders, be they of yesterday, today, or the future. The community alone is aware of the problems of its members. The Boko/mbôngi can undertake any project for the welfare of its members.

8) "Lusânga didi dia kimvuka." The lusanga/boko is the center, think tank of community activities

(mvemono). Outside of this "didi dia kimvuka," man's activities are sterile.

9) "Yèmba wayembamana mâmbu ma kânda." It is the boko that covers community affairs. The community covers more than what one can say.

10) "N'samu katoma ku kiôto; kabîya ku kiôto." All solutions are possible at ku boko. Conflicts are not discussed outside of the community institutions.

11) "Kiôto kiôko kia kânda kalâmbanga." It is the boko that cooks community inhalation. The community healing meal is made at the boko. The boko is the healer of community diseases, problems of all orders.

The short list of these Kôngo proverbs shows how the Boko is an important social institution among the Bântu-Kôngo, where only public and community affairs are discussed. To speak about private affairs in this public institution, yèmba, is a public crime. One does not plot inside Kôngo public institutions. It is interesting to notice here that the external part of a house, veranda, among the Kôngo is called yèmba, i.e., the public part of the house. This part is for public use, to sit, work, gather, take shelter or even sleep under it. The owner of the house has no right against those acts. Another very interesting Kôngo proverb/principle says "What you think belongs to you, but what you say belongs to the public," [Ma ku nsia n'-tima, mâku; matèle, ma ku mbazi.]. Inside you are you;

outside you are not. You are only a tiny part of a huge and coherent body, the community within the universal totality.

The community council of elders [mfûndu a mbuta za vata] meets in the boko. Their duties are to review and discuss all questions related to the community life and submit their proposals to the community assembly of honored elders [fôngo dia mfumu ye ngânga za vata]. Members of the community council are sent to the community assembly. The boko is also the center, didi, of cultural information. It is here that research or study on social problems is done. It is here also that new members in the community, visitors, make their first step toward integration in the community. All personal and political alliances are made in the boko in public view and by public accord. All decisions made ku boko have "force de loi" (force of the law).

When the community assembly [fôngo dia vata] meets, delegations from other communities are free to participate in the assembly in the interest of their own communities. Here each belo, as a delegation, carefully handles all pertinent questions concerning the community life.

In any assembly, the community delegations can discuss all issues pertaining to community except the three issues of community/clan, land, taboo (Kânda, N'toto, Kîna). The community land is untouchable, it is considered taboo [kîna or n'lôngo] because it belongs first to the eternal community roots, the ancestors, (the real living gods) as well as to the people in the living community. Traditionally every assembly must start with alternatively repeated mottoes called "bikûmu" (Fu-Kiau 1973):

Kûmbisi: Kîna kia n'toto!
Kûmbi: Kîna kia nsi
Kûmbisi: Kîna kia nsi!
Kûmbi: Kîna kia n'kângu!
Kûmbisi: Kîna kia n'kângu!
Kûmbi: Ndefi tûka mu bakulu!
Kûmbisi: E n'singa-dikânda!
Kûmbi: Nînga ka tabuka ko!

Leader: The land taboo!
Audience: Country's taboo!
Leader: Country's taboo!
Audience: People's taboo!
Leader: People's taboo!
Audience: Infallible oath!
Leader: What about the community's bio-string!
Audience: It must be strengthened, not be cut down (weakened)!

These very powerful dialectical aphorisms and chants are used by the Bântu-Kôngo when publically dealing with serious situations menacing a structurally fundamental, social organization or institution, such as boko or a public good such as land. Such "Kûmu", dialectic aphorisms, are considered to be public legal oaths, and at the same time, become social taboos, i.e., as Balikci states, "The first automatic defense mechanism against uncontrollable and unpredictable dangers" (Balikci, 1970:223). Defense mechanism values of N'singa-dikânda's accumulate by the community in the course of time. The n'singa-dikânda is the moral, social, spiritual, cultural, and physical link between community members, but also between them and their ancestors, the eternal root not only of life, but also of the law. The n'singa-dikânda is the biological string that links all community members, dead or alive, to both ends of the rope.

Through its community council and community assembly, the Kôngo society makes its laws and trains its youth for national and community defense. Because the army had to serve the community's interest, it was the responsibility of all people to educate their young men and women. "In the Kôngo there was no real standing army. Soldiers were recruited by general mobilization" (Kajsa, 1978:79). The army in the old Kôngo was by and for all people. The main mission of such a populist army was to kick all enemies out of the ancestral taboo lands. The defense of the land was and still is the cornerstone of oral and unwritten legislation. One who knows the Kôngo land holding system, knows its social organization, and therefore its concept of law and crime in the past as well as the present.

The Ancestral Land

One of the essential characteriestics of the Kôngo system of property is its inalienability. There is no valuable condition that could change this inalienability of the ancestral land. "Land was not a commodity to be bought and sold. Land was inalienable in the traditional system. Each domain was owned by a certain matrilineage which could indeed grant the use of a part of its area to a relative or even foreign matrilineage, but this did not mean that it gave up its land rights." (Kajsa, 1978, p 71). In their fu-kia-nsi, the unwritten law, the traditional land system, the Kôngo say to sell community land is to carry a mortal yoke[Wateka n'toto wa kânda neti ngôroro/vangu]. Malengreau also wrote about this same concept of the inalienability of the land among other Bântu people of the Congo basin. He says that the African communalistic concept of society was based on a very strong law, that of "the indivisisbility and the inalienability of the land" (cited by Muller, 1956:13). Whoever does not have access to land is dead; no matter how rich he/she is.

Contrary to what is happening in the Modern African puppet states, with a few exceptions among the more progressive countries, "The chief of the community is not the landlord, but only a manager of the interests of the community of which he is the head, (Muller, 1956). That is why it was almost impossible to corrupt a true African societal leader as the Kôngo will say the community leader is uncorrubtible for he knows kinswèkila, corruption, is a pitfall to the community and to the country, Mfumu-dikânda katâmbulanga kinswèkila ko, n'tâmbu kwa kânda ye nsi]. Today, kinswèkila (embezzlement) has becine currrent money among leaders in Africa. When Africans talk about what oral traditions say about land ownership, most scholars, bought by capitalist-imperialist companies and corporations, often reply that they do not trust unrecorded traditions; they totally ignore what their friends, other fellow scholars, have recorded about the African concept of land ownership. There are many documents by western writers and reporters on African oral traditions related to the issue of land ownership. Most of them point out the upholding of this concept throughout most African societies and communities as one Africanist scholar writes, "The clan possesses lands in title of occupation and of use, i.e., to live on it and for it. The right of occupation and the right of use belong, not to the chief of the clan but to the entire collectivity" (DeCleene, 1946:25).

Capitalist-imperialist forces did not understand the African concept of the land holding. European colonial exploitation introduced the theory of "vacant land" in Africa ignoring totally, as Malengreau (cited in Muller, 1956:10) states that "The territory is the property of the community . . . vacant territory does not exist." The uncultivated lands left in the natural process of refertilization according to the African traditional rotary system were seen by Europeans as wasted and vacant lands. The African rotary system was instituted in order to avoid the impoverishment of the soil in a continent, such as Africa, with a very harsh and drastic climate. Without knowing the reason for what they saw and believed as a precarious abandonment of the land, they seized it because they had firearms and made it "vacant." Due to the possession of arms and agressive technology, the colonization ordered the expropriation and relocation of native communities. They declared all of what was believed to be vacant land the state's land, i.e., the property of European settlers, the colonialists. It was by this process that the illegal and minority govenments of Southern Africa seized the lands they occupy today, where they built the most inhumane governmental system that man has experienced since the beginning of time: the western, Christian, apartheid system (in Zimbabwe and in Azania).

The Congo Free State, freed from western penetration through an ordinance on July 1, 1885, gave the mining company of UMHK (Mining Union of Higher Katanga) an area larger than half the size of Belgium. Many other domains and concessions were also freely distributed to other allies of imperialism (Kajsa, 1972:73). Lemarchande states the same view "Thousands of acres were given to missionaries, private companies and settlers." (Lemarchande, 1964:11). Only good and fertile land was expropriated. Land was also automatically expropriated at any time once a mineral was found on it. This expropriation of good, fertile, and rich soil, between 1910 to 1930, became the principal cause of malnutrition, disease, the increase of the death rate, and a rural exodus. The transfer of African community land to capitalistic and private ownership was the key to the destruction of the traditional African institutions of law and justice. This same factor became, since 1950 to the present, the main cause of struggle on the African continent, the struggle to free taboo ancestral land from the hands of corporations and their allies.

The existing legislature in Africa cannot free the African people because that legislature is sterile and alienated from its true cultural and environmental milieu. It is not rooted within the people's culture. As Yabila says "The law becomes sterile when one separates it from its milieu" (Yabila, 1974:78). Its primary goal is to defend existing and future adventurists' properties and interests in African land, the people's land which is a taboo ancestral land. There needs to be a radical change in this legislature today because "The law is not only a science, a set of techniques of analysis, but a vehicle of culture" (Yabila, 1974:79). That law, in order to be take root in African society and serve as a cultural vehicle, must rise from within the people's culture. The law must speak the same language spoken by the people and be written in that language. All modern African constitutions and laws are written in foreign languages—the fact that they are written in languages unknown by the majority of the African populations, is already depriving the African masses of one of their most important rights, that of knowing their law. To understand the law fairly, exactly and completely is a human right. African laws are not, in that case, written for the African people, they are written for those who are interested in exploiting Africa and its people in order to facilitate their tasks, that of underdeveloping Africa.

In certain countries only 1% of the entire population could read and understand the official language in which laws are written (Fu-Kiau, 1969a:12). In many African countries, documents, newspapers, and books related to governmental activities often are not allowed to be sold in the country. They are kept in secrecy from the citizens, but exploitative companies and corporations have all rights of access to them. This fact shows and proves that most African governments work as agencies of foreign governments.

Changes in matter of law are almost impossible in Africa because of the state of African parliaments existing there today "The parliament as it is . . . retards the application of vital decisions and does not play its role of guardian of the public interest" (Young, 1965:355).

African parliaments cannot function with efficacity for the people's well being because of the external influences which always try to "buy" all sons of the continent who are supposed to be responsible for it. This situation has gotten worse for the case of Zaire since the withdrawal of the UN army forces in 1963. The removal of the international forces from the Congo (Zaire) gave way to a new situation: Neo-colonization and its intensification. The country found itself in a situation where it could find no solution to its problems. As Young says "There are no doubt solutions, but no one among them leads automatically to success because in all circumstances the external influence became again more and more important since the retreat of the UN forces (Young, 1965:356). As such, internal struggles will continue in Africa until change in the interest of the masses occurs.

The African masses fight today because their present leaders continue to follow the path of a very negative capitalism, which is not their way of life. This capitalism results in crimes against innocent and peaceful people by preventing them access to their ancestral tabooed land and the joy of liberty; the liberty of political participation. The African masses see the behavior of their leaders as a public crime. They will be judged as well as their supporters.

Crime

One talks about "committing a crime" in western judiciary language. But in most African cultures, and that of the Kôngo in particular, one says "Nata n'kanu," bearing a crime. One must discuss the contrast between these two concepts in order to more easily understand the African concept of crime. This distinction is basically linguistico-cultural. Understanding "les-jeux-des-mots", wordgames, is very important in any study of two or more distinct cultures. A wordgame is a key word to intellectual or scientific understanding. In English one "feels a pain"; in Kongolese (Kikôngo), one "sees a pain," [mona mpasi]. When an Englishman "smokes a cigarette," a Mukôngo will "drink a cigarette" [nwa saka/nsûnga]. In English one "smells a certain perfume," the Mukôngo will "hear it" [wa nsûnga]. When western school defines man as "an intelligent animal, an imperial animal" or as a "toolmaker," as do the non-initiated African scholars, the westernized, i.e., the "kiyînga" in the African way of thinking; the "Ngânga," the intitated African man in the African way of thinking, who is a specialist of perceiving the world's things, will, himself prefer to say that the human being is a system of systems [Mûntu i kimpa kia bimpa]. He is also variably called "n'kîngu a n'kîngu"—a principle of princples, i.e., the pattern of patterns. Because "mûntu," the human being, is the key system of systems, he is able as such to produce materially and technologically other mechanical systems[1]. For the Bântu, in accordance to the concept expressed in the Kôngo language, man is not an animal, nor is he comparable to one, "mûntu," the human being has the dual [mwèla-ngîndu]

1. For more information about Bântu-Kôngo thought, read the forth coming book by Fu-Kiau, Makuku Matatu.

soul-mind that distinguishes him from the rest of the things of nature[2] [ma-bia-nsemono].

When the physical body dies, says a Mûntu, the dual [mwèla-ngindu] of that being remains within the community or out of it. The dual of the being [Mwèla-ngîndu], continues to act and to talk to and among the community's members as well as to the world's community, through dreams and visions, waves, radiations, and through monumental acts: the biological, material, intellectual and spiritual treasures accumulated in scrolls [ku mpèmba], the past, i.e., the perpetual bank of the generating/driving forces of life. (See figure 17). There is no end in the dingo-dingo process, the perpetual going-and-coming-back of life as well as in the Mûntu's [mwèla-ngîndu]. Life is a continuum through many stages (as discussed in Makuku Matatu). For the Bântu, there is no death and no resurrection; for them life is a continual proces of change. An animal's life [zîngu kia bulu/môyo a bulu] does not have the dual [mwèla-ngîndu] soul-mind. It does not follow the process because the animal is not a system of systems [kimpa kia bimpa]: it's not a vertical being, it is a prostrated being. Animals are horizontal beings, they move and act instinctually. The mûntu, human being, is a V-H-being [kadi kiatelama lwîmbangânga va lukôngolo]. He stands vertically on his feet first, he thinks and reasons before moving horizontally to meet the challenges of life and of the world.

These differences in feeling, thinking and perceiving are

2. The translation of Mûntu as a person or human being is more accurate than the word "man," which has its equivalents as "bakala, mobali, jend" in certain Bântu languages.

Figure 20.

similar to the concepts of social and structural organization. Outside of the expressions "drink tobacco" [nwa saka], pull tobacco [benda fûmu], suck tobacco [wèla nsûnga], and [tompisa fumu] smoke or fire tobacco, it is almost impossible to find in English the correct conceptual meaning a Mukôngo gives to the term smoke in his or her tongue. This tells us how impossible it is to impose a new system that cannot possibly fit on a people who already have their own system of thought. In the west one believes that he/she is born with his knowing power (IQ). The African individual who is intitiated to principles of life and living will say no. Knowledge (IQ) is not in us. Knowledge is outside of us. The only thing we have in us is the power to shelve the information or data in us and reproduce it at will. One cannot dance with ease in a borrowed wrap (N'lele ansômpa ka utominanga makinu ko). It is wrong for one system to try to manipulate or impose one's way of thinking upon other systems. Such an attempt only worsens the world's relationships, a confirmation of the total lack of know how in the area of, knotting (coding) and unknotting (decoding) in one's own life [kânga ye kutula mu luzîngu]. But let us go back to the concept of crime.

In the western concept, the individual seems to be responsible for his crime. He is either conscious or unconscious of it; it is only committed by him. The western expression "to commit a crime" does not seem to have any historic or cultural implication. But in the case of the Kôngo, the expression, to bear a crime [nata n'kanu], there are cultural, linguistic, social, environmental, and genetic/biologic roots. The individual, before committing any crime, carries a certain set of learned criminal concepts, images, expressions, symbols, discussions, words, habits, and facts upon diverse social scenes. In other words, for the Bântu, a crime is the result of an internal psychological state carried by an individual since his childhood, mainly accumulated during the period of growth when the child acquires social patterns. That state is given to him by his social, cultural, physical, and systematic environment within which he is bathed by negative as well as positive waves/radiations [minika/minienie].

Crimes are not individual acts. They are, in many cases, earlier social creations which do not appear until later, at the moment they are committed by an individual who only is the symptomatic furuncle of the criminal radiations accumulated within the society.

Crimes are found within social and cultural patterns; in the food and in the way a society eats that food; in its taboos; in its language, and the vocabulary used to communicate concepts, ideas, and values; in the way alien cultures are interpreted, and in the way social, cultural and ideological discrepancies are understood.

Before he goes to initiation [ku kânga, ku kôngo or ku

lônde] (Africa) or to school (other societies), the child learns such concepts as steal, kill, lie, sin, rich, poor, minority, foreign, mine, yours, illogical people, reserved for green people only, etc. It is through this kind of socialization that the concept of crime is transmitted to members of a particular cultural system. Societies as well as systems prepare their own foes and their own underminers. Crimes are foes and underminers of societies and systems. They are the conduct of societies and systems. The repetition of a criminal act shows how bad a system is. Crime, for the Bântu-Kôngo, is a learned behavior, and it is possible to eradicate it from human society.

To teach young men any word that has a negative connotation for the community is regarded as injecting criminal roots within the community. The African people and the Kôngo in particular, believe that the reason for committing a crime is relative to the crime and social or cultural system in which he lives. In other words, a social system either favors or does not favor crime. In pouring war-like toys in our communities, children are engaged in the easiest process of learning how to commit crimes. In other words, the war-like toys' industry has industrialized crimes within human society.

When a crime is committed, judgment should not only be passed on to the criminal, but also on to the entire community in which the crime found its roots. A community in which a man or a woman poisons his or her spouse would have trouble finding new alliances with other communities, and one will say to such a community: Be aware that that community gives poison by all means [kânda diôdio ndîkila bavânanga]. As a consequence, nobody will shake hands anymore with someone from that community; nobody will politically deal with such a community; nobody will seek water in such a community; nobody will dream to marry in such a community no matter how beautiful the youngsters are in that community; and nobody will seek a good friend in that community. Such a social behavior among the Kôngo tells how the crime is not seen as an individual act, but as a social one. If the poison used was developed within the community for other reasons other than killing, the community, its holders of the community [sîmbi bia kimvuka], will develop a strong social and legal ethic about the use of that poison.

In a society in which people believe in the concept of bearing crimes before possibly committing them, punishment is first considered communal before being an individual matter, and as a consequence the elders discipline on the young is very important.

The Kôngo society is a good example of a society whose entire social structure is basically a taboo system. The most important taboos are those related to the land, goods from that land, and all matter related to the community name. As such, most of what are considered crimes are related to the issue of land, the source of all goods for the survival of life.

a) Crimes concerning the land

We have already said above that the right of land ownership belongs only to the community. No one in the community could claim private ownership to any position of the land. To own or sell land is considered one of the most serious crimes that an individual may commit, crimes for which he may not be forgiven by community members. Land, because it is an inviolable taboo, should remain in the service of all community members.

During his lifetime a community member has the right to harvest his fields and fruit trees, but after his death, the land and all property on that land, i.e., fruit trees, houses, industries, farms, etc. go back to community ownership. This kind of property inherited by the community, according to the basic concept and taboo of the inalienability of the land, is called fwa-dia-kânda. The fwa-dia-kânda is an accumulated heritage that enforces community control of land and all properties related to it. These properties constitute the basic sources of kânda's common-wealth [mvwîlu a kânda] also called kimvwâma kia kânda or mayudukwa ma kânda used to solve kânda's diverse problems [lânda n'samu mia nsi ye mia kânda] or to assist community members in time of need.

b) Individual wealth is an abominable crime

Individual wealth of all kinds above the accepted standard of necessary goods, is considered a crime. One says that this kind of wealth could not be accumulated without exploiting [wuka/yiba] other members of the community. In that case, the wealth itself is called kimvwâma kia muyeke, wealth that betrays, yekula, the community and its members. The owner of such excessive properties was often killed or hoodooed [lokwa]. African communities believe strongly that the individual accumulation of property has always had negative effects on the traditional social structure and on policy-making institutions.

The traditional social system of the Kôngo does not permit rich people to lead national or community institutions because a proverb says a rich man never talks or fights for other people's interest unless it is to further his own interests. [Mvwâma nsusu; kanwâna, mâki mândi katânini]. That is why traditionally, wealth does not play a role in either the social ranking system or alliance making among the Bântu (Muller, 1956:8). This situation is changing today because the same rich individuals have the power to buy guns which give them not only more power, but the license to kill whoever they declare as dangerous. Firing squads are increasing throughout the African continent, not of criminals, but of innocent individuals who are challenging corrupt practices of politicians.

c) To misrepresent his kimvuka is a political crime

A Kôngo proverb says politics is a community matter; the individual does not make community policies, for individual policy was unknown since the time of the ancestors [Kinzônzi kia kânda; kia kingenga bakulu (ka) basîsa kio ko]. The individual does not make community policies says another Kôngo proverb one mouth is an empty calabash [N'nwa mosi tutu]. Kôngo traditional thought explains clearly that all people develop and direct community policies. Individuals do not make policy even though they are allowed to represent the community by delegation. An individual who is going to represent the community policy is publicly tested before being sent on any diplomatic mission. If he fails by misrepresenting the community he is buried alive in a public place, generally in the market place, zându (Munzele, 1965).

To misrepresent the people or the community insists Mbuta Munzele in his marvelous book on Kôngo traditions, is to compromise the future of the community. In order to show the seriousness of such a political crime, in accordance to the law, the criminal was buried alive publicly in the market place. Before his burial, the criminal made a public statement of his crime, gave advice to future representatives of the community policy and diplomacy, and thereafter he was thrown alive in a burial hole. Mbuta Munzele clearly tells us that his diplomatic mission [kintumwa kia maghûbi /kinimalônde] was one of the most dangerous functions. Failure in such a mission led straight to a cruel and inevitable death.

Political and diplomatic missions were akin to deification for those who knew how to handle the people's responsbility. Coming back from an important and successful mission for my community, a sîmbi kia nsi, literally, holder of the country's equilibrium, a wise man took my hands, spit on them, and said: "If you season the policy of people and the community correctly, you are deified" [Watwîsa mûngwa ye nûngu mu kinzôzi kia n'kângu ye kânda, zâmbusu]. This Kôngo proverb shows us that only obedience to the people's will makes people heroes and gods and not otherwise for the red carpet is not requested, it is earned [nkwâl'a luzitu ka yilômbwanga ko].

Because of the embodiment of this concept of others before oneself, the Bântu's daily expression tends to eliminate the subjective and egoistic use of "I" when dealing with important social issues. They prefer to build their thought on "ancestral" basis, i.e., historic and taboo basis, the accumulated knowledge and experience: the ancestors in their experience have said or the past says [Bakulu bata ngana] or [Bambuta bata ngana]; according to ancestors' law [Ngana yata bambuta]; the spiritual holders of the country have said [Sîmbi bia nsi vo]; accordingly to the unwritten law, the traditional constitutions [Lândila fu-kia-nis]; Country's practices, norms, values, patterns, and systems do not say it [Kisinsi ka kitèle bo ko], etc. All these expressions are judiciary, legal and sententious expressions mainly used in public statements, or to fit ones own thought within the framework of social patterns and values, but also to avoid culpability before the law and public condemnation of selfishness. There is no creation outside of people. Pretended individual creation, according to Kôngo thought, is a lie and a social crime: creations are collective works, because they are people's accumulated thoughts [Mpângulu mayîndu mantotikisa]. In other words, they germinate from collective ideas. Notice here that the period in which proverbs were created [tându kiatewa ngana], is a broad historical period that transpires before colonization; a period in which the African Mûntu was able to think and create freely. There is a huge split between that period and the present time in Africa. The present Africa "swims" within a period without "ngana," (principles, theories, concepts or systems), this is a period of the oppressed man, i.e., the man without a brain, a brainwashed man. This is the suffering Africa, because it goes against, autocritique and collective dialectics [ntungasani ye kinzônzi], its own concepts.

For the Bântu, and the Kôngo in particular, it is a crime to own property that is worth more than the standard wealth of ordinary members of the community. Such property could not be obtained by honest means without taking the path of exploiting the community and its members [wuka kimvuka ye bièla biândi]. Here is a widespread aphorism that community members sing (cite) before a meeting that deals with serious social, political, economic or criminal issues within the community (excerpt from Makuku Matutu).

Mu kânda
Within the community
Ka mukadi mputu
There is no room for poverty
Mu kânda
Within the community
Ka mukadi mvwâma
There is no room for ill obtained wealth
Mu kânda
Within the community
Ka mukadi mpofo
There is no room for blindness
Mu kânda
Within the community
Ka mukadi mfumu
There is no room for "order-giver"
Ka mukadi n'nânga
There is no room for slaves
Babo mfumu na mfumu
All are masters, and only masters
Babo ngânga na ngânga
All specialists, and only specialists

Mu kânda
Within the community
Bilesi
Young generations
Mu kânda
Within the community
Mwâna mfumu
Ancestors' sons
Mu kânda
Within the community
Busi/nsâng'a kânda
A sister, the community shoot
Mu kânda
Within the community
Nkasi a kânda
A brother, the future leader

Mu kânda
Within the community
Kinenga ye dedede
Equilibrium and equality
Mu kânda
Within the community
Kingenga/kimpambudi mwânana
There is no room for separatism/privacy
Mu kânda
Within the community
Sèkila kumosi
All sleep at once
Mu kânda
Within the community

Sikamana kumosi
All wake up at once
Mu kânda
Within the community
Mbèni ku mbazi
Enemies stand out

This very poetic and political aphorism of folk teaching demonstrates how the dialectical philosophy of "primitive" African collectivism is rooted among African societies in general, and among the Bântu in particular. African collectivism practised among the Bântu-Kôngo rejects poverty as well as private ownership of property such as land, industries, means of production, etc. Such properties should only be owned and controlled by the community. The attention in this community is more centered on man as part of a body, the community, [kânda/mumvuka]. As such, that part must obey the community law, and not the contrary of that n'kîngu, principle. The Kôngo concept of wealth and kânda does not mean that the Kôngo reject the practical money value; they, of course, do need money within the community to serve its members, not to oppress them, for they say—When you engender offspring, you must also engender the material goods to secure their life [Wabuta, buta na mbôngo].

Debate Process

According to Kôngo: social, political, economic, and judiciary matters must be discussed publicly. This concept is confirmed by the frequent use of two proverbs: There is no privacy in affairs [Kingenga kia mâmbu kwanâna], and for want of going alone, the river is curved [Nto wayenda bukaka wakôndama]. All problems related to man within this context are social, economic, and political. And all social, economic, and political problems are problems of the peoples' interest; they should be discussed publicly to instruct both idiot and intelligent individuals [Mazoba ye bandwènga balwèngila mo].

The existence of public courts [Mbasi-a-n'kanu or fundusulu] among the Bântu exemplifies how community life was more important than that of a particular individual despite the material wealth he has, "Wealth does not play a role in the social ranking system, or in alliance making." (Muller, 1956:8). Human and communal values are more important than all the property a rich man may possess.

When conflict occurs within the community, the eldest of elder leaders calls for a public hearing/meeting with a general delay of one to two weeks if the issue does not need an immediate solution (the Kôngo traditional week had four days). He may urge that the meeting take place sooner, if it is a serious situation. This meeting always takes place beneath the shadow of a tree under which the court of judgment [Kiânzala kia mfundusulu] is arranged. Under this tree experts investigate the issue at hand, its ramifications, and its effects on the community life. The debate is carried on dialectically through diverse songs, slogans, proverbs, aphorisms, calls and responses followed by comments. The accused is seated within the circle and any community member is allowed to ask this person questions. The main goal of this procedural investigation is to understand social problems and conflicts through the accused and therefore try to find a remedy to cure him as well as the entire community [nzila mu lâmba kiôko/kiôto kia kânda].

When the discussion of the case is over, two commissions [mfûndu] are set up. The first, a commision of decision [mfûndu za luzèngo], and the second, a commission of social reintegration [mfûndu za lutambudulu or mfûndu za bindôkila]. The first commission is established specially to take judicial measure fitting the case, e.g., death in case of extreme violation of communal law and taboo. This commission is only composed of men and women considered as outstanding dialecticians/judges [Zônzi biakafu-kafu], and whose names are chosen because of their interest in the total defense of the community and the inalienability of the ancestral land.

The second commission [mfûndu za lutambudulu] or the reintegration ritual commission is more ethical than the judiciary one. Its mission is to find out means and a process by which social balance will be reestablished and its law reinforced. But also, in the case of small infractions, to establish a ritual process by which the guilty or the deviant will be reintegrated in the community life by the ritual of forgiveness [Yambudila] (Fu-Kiau, 1969:68–70) or, in the case of a criminal, how he will be healed or punished.

Each commission gives, orally and in detail, a complete report to the public. It is up to the public to accept or to reject the commission's proposed decision. In case of public rejection, the case is left, very often, in the hands of the elders and the decision made by these men and women is rarely rejected. It is said to be very frightening anytime the womens' side favors a strong decision.

Elders, in the Kôngo judiciary structure, form the highest body of justice, the court, [mbasi-a-n'kanu]; in other words, judiciary institutions in the Kôngo system are communal and independant. The king's duties were more diplomatic, martial, and monetary rather than internal administration, "Each community was a real state within the kingdom" (Fu-Kiau 1973).

The Kôngo concept of law and crime as described here is not well known by the outside world, even by those who were their oppressors, the former colonial masters. This ignorance is due to two main factors: (1) The ethnocentrism of the western world as built upon the colonial phenomenon which is seen as "The domination of a native majority by a minority of foreigners in the name of racial and cultural superiority" (Balandier, cited in William, 1972:8). This notion of racial and cultural superiority prevented the colonialists from objectively seeing the cultural values of the colonized. (2) Colonial masters had a different goal in Africa contrary to the one often stated as the "Mission of civilization." Their goal was and still is the exploitation of natural wealth or resources in order to further their own economy back home. "There is no development here, but only commercial exploitation of natural wealth" (William, 1972:10), and he continues "To sum up, all aspects of the . . . venture were subordinated to purely economic consideration. The educational system produced the skilled and semi-skilled workers needed for the exploitation of the Congo, while missionary organizations installed in these same workers a morality based on order and authority. Because of these goals conlonialism-imperialism did all in its power to destroy African cultures and traditions (what it continues through present African leaders) in order to deepen its racist and exploitative philosophy that left the heritage problems faced in Africa today. Fortunately they were not able to destroy the African "vibrating rolls/knots" of the period of thinkers [tându kiatewa ngana] which are accumulated "ku mpèmba, the perpetual bank of driving forces of life.

Yet Africa is in conflict today because of these artificial structures established by artificial African law, a law that is against the will of the African people. Africa struggles because it seeks to cut itself away from all the exploitative chains it is tied to. All investments, properties, concessions, etc. granted today in Africa under the present artificial law, are not secure for African systematic way of organization [Kimpa kia kisinsi] will not tolerate such departures from our kisinsi, the African way of life organization, and because these proprietorships support present inhumane regimes throughout Africa. Sooner or later Africa will uncover, through cultural driving forces, its taboo principles, the law of the inalienability of the ancestral land, etc. Whatever capitalism or communism may do in Africa by corrupting its leaders, Africa will never adopt any of these systems because none of them, in all their betterment, could fit well in Africa. The African future will be built on its own norms and values that are deep-rooted in its own systems, which are unfortunately unknown by the great majority of its leaders, our African Kisinsi. Since this system is not discussed scholarly elsewhere, it seems important to me, before ending this chapter, to describe shortly what makes the main difference between this system and other systems, i.e., capitalism and socialism/communism [Kinyudiki/Kimayudukwa ye Kimumvuka/Kikintwâdi].

Capitalism, on a national level, is a system whereby the work of the majority of people produce the wealth for a few individuals who are owners of means of production. On an international level, capitalism is a system by which the world's developing countries provide the work and raw materials, to make the wealthy minority gain. In other words, the slavery of man by man is the basic source of capitalism and its expansion in the world. This capitalistic view is different from the communistic one. Communism, on the contrary, is a system that tries to control in the name of the state the wealth and the land of a given country pretending equality among its citizens. These two systems, capitalism and communism/socialism are, by all means, in the African view equally imperialistic systems. These two systems are the cause of the world's insecurity because of their superficial antagonism. Because of the lack of their mutual understanding they are destructors of international institutions, and above all, they are killers of the world's order and its leaders. They are indeed "oiseaux de même plumage" (birds of the same feather) whatever their tensions are. Neither system lives without their hand on the gun because they only own by the art of killing.

Contrary to capitalism and communism/socialism, the African "Kisinsi" is different. What the Bântu-Kôngo, Luba, Mongo, Nyarwanda, Zulu, etc., constitute in their daily life is a system [kimpa/fu] whereby the land, source of happiness and blessing to all terrestrial life, belongs not to individuals, landlords, or to a state, as it respectively exists in the case of capitalistic and communalistic systems, but to the essential fundamental community, kânda, and all its members, be they poor, rich, scholars, idiots, young or elder. They all have full access to that inalienable land. As a Kôngo proverb says, "Community land is our life" [N'toto wa kânda ni môyo èto].

The Kisinsi is a system by which the chief is a symbol, the mâmbu, (literally words, affairs, policy) belong to the people of the community (society) in its entirety. In the African system, Kisinsi, the individual is never a land belonging to heirs. The right to heritage belongs to the community only. The African Kisinsi is explicit here by the Kôngo society, that it is a system where leadership is a moving force [Kimfumu ma kiantûmba] held through the "stooling" process [mu ntûmbulu] under the control of all social forces throughout their political, philosophical, religious, and productive relationships in all locative levels, conceptually and cosmologically generated here (see figures 6 through 17) from Kala, emerging life level and its growth towards leadership, to Tukula, present authorities' level and its leadership; from Tukula, through Luvèmba, the step for greatest change and for abandonment of all negative accumulated elements within the system, to Musoni, the social jinn, [sîmbi bia nsi], the step for regeneration of forces, potentialities, and vitality needed to reshape and rebuild the system, i.e. the rebirth of the process, or the dingo-dingo, the constant back and forth flow of energy of change. On the basis of these cosmological ideas, the concept of dictatorship is impossible in the African Kôngo-Kisinsi discussed here through its cosmological ideas.

The Kôngo-Kisinsi is a conceptual system which is aware of Mwisikânda, the human community members, rather than about outsiders' interests [n'luta mia banzènza]. Kisinsi, a strong and fundamental African system that would build a strong Kisafelika, is not a chauvinistic system of philosophy. The Kisinsi is a huge tree which strongly emphasizes first, a positively peaceful and fraternal neighborhood among all its branches: On Kisafelika and Bisafelika, strong neighborhood in continental states and their inhabitants; on Kisinsi, strong neighborhood within the national diversities; on Kisikânda, strong neighborhood in the ethnic groups and communities; on Kisizûnga, strong neighborhood in local communities; on Kisivata, strong neighborhood in the village's subdivisions such as belo, mwèlonzo, môyo and buta[3]. The Kisinsi deals with all mûntu, human beings, as part of the human race and its community survival.

The Kisinsi is a system of philosophy fundamentally based on tolerance. The Kisinsi punishes with care and

[3] The particle "kisi" is a prefix meaning norms, values, beliefs, system belonging to. Don't confuse this prefix with the prefix "ki" preceding proper nouns which means tongue of or doctrine set up by, philosophy of, e.g. Kikôngo (language of Kôngo people, Bakôngo); Kiswahili (language of Waswahili); Kisokrate (doctrine, theory or philosophy of Sokrate: Socratism); Kikimbangu (doctrine set up by Kimbangu:Kimbanguism, 1921); Kilenine (doctrine and theory of or about Lenine: Leninism); Kiklisto (Christism, not Christianism); Kibaklisto (christianism).

love; it regulates social conflicts in the ways of love and autocraticism [zola ye ntungasani]. As a member of Kisinsi, a Mwisinsi does not arm himself against another mûntu, because he himself is a mûntu, a being under the control of the dual soul-mind. He wants to see in all freedom other soul-minds develop in other bodies as in one's self in order to live [zînga, i.e., tâmbula ye tambikisa] receiving and passing on. Because systems do not have the dual [mwèla-ngîndu] by themselves, they become worse when led by leaders whose soul-mind development is under the lowest level of human value understanding. The Kisinsi, as kimpa/system in bad hands, becomes a killer and does kill.

Mûntu, the soul-mind-object [ma kia mwèla ye nitu], should not kill other soul-mind-objects as a respect to himself and to his bumûntu (mindfulness). When a mûntu, in whatever intention, kills another mûntu, he looses his state of inner human being [mbèlo a kimûntu], i.e., that of the soul-mind-object. He identifies himself with an animal, the no-soul-mind-object. Then he loses his verticality [kintombayulu], the power to think before making any decision, to yield for horizontality [kilukôngolo], the power to act instinctively as do all prostrated beings.

The act of killing soul-mind-objects is the strongest factor that reveals not only the weakness of a leader, but also his complex of inferiority and all kinds of psychological problems it may reveal. This is, in short, the main ideas that explain the Kisinsi upon which the African concept of law and crime discussed in this chapter find their roots. It is upon this sytem that Africa is going to build its future with its doors largely open not only to its "best friends", if they do exist, but to all its enemies, because they are well known, for they are constituted as human beings, i.e., naturally, rightly and legally co-owners of our planetary land.

African leaders must see today's world policy differently in order to understand carefully from the bottom of their hearts the role that Africa should play in the future of the human beings that we all are, for the peace of this world. African leaders should deeply understand that the continent they are leading today has a special mission. A mission that should develop a new order which will save humanity and this world. As a Negro Slave, Hollis Read, wrote more than a century ago, "Africa has been reserved for the development of a higher order of civilization."[4] Such an order and responsibility will never be conceived by the awakening of Africa if its leaders continue to follow the path of present world tensions based on ideological antagonisms, and, moreover, if African leaders found African nations upon personal prestige, corruption, human torture, inconceivable expenditures, meaningless projects rather than seeking solutions to real, social problems posed throughout the continent among its inhabitants: Housing, nutrition, water, disease, education, transportation, poverty, rural exodus, and agricultural development.

I think it is a social crime for any African authority "paying" himself, say $5,000 monthly in a country with an economic system where more than 90% of the citizens, because of the poor national planning policy, live with less than $100 for the entire year. Today's African leaders do

[4]. H. Read, 1864: *The Nego Problem Solved*, p. 25.

not seem to be paid. They go as many times as they want to the national bank and "load" trunks of their cars with any amount of money they desire. For them every weekday is a payday. It is a universal shame for foreign governments to support such policies, whatever be their interests, in such corrupted, undemocratic and bankrupted nations. The fall of such governments will weigh more on their supporters rather than on the supported individuals themselves.

To Africans of all ages it is about time to rethink what the Kôngo ancestors aphorismically said once "Don't allow the exploitation to repeat itself" [Nkutu a zèngi fwânda lumbu kimosi].

Proverbs Used Within the Community About the Community

Ngana zitewanga mu kânda mu diâmbu dia kânda

When the African in general, and the Kongolese [N'kôngo] in particular, uses the expression "bambuta bata ngana" or "ngana yata bambuta/kingana kiata bambuta" literally proverbs/theories said by ancestors - he refers, according to the context to a philosophical, social, dialectical, theoretical, legal or judiciary statement. In that case bambuta bata ngana may explicitly refer to one among the following explanations:

According to the unwritten law of our society
Accordingly to the law
Accordingly to the custom

According to the ancient theory
Conformity to the law
Conformity to the social patterns, norms and values
In accordance to the well known cases
Conformity to our principles
The law says
In accordance to the exigencies of the system
Let's consult the law
Our concept of the law tells us that
Legally that means . . .
Legally speaking . . .
Judiciary speaking . . .
The law says
The law is . . . etc.

The proverb is one among the most important sources that best explain the African Mûntu and his thought. In debates, in ceremonies, in judgments, in joy as well as in misery, proverbs are freqeuntly used to reprimand, to criticize, to compare, to segregate, to encourage, to punish, and to heal. They are used to teach, to explain and to thoroughly code and decode [kânga ye kutula].

For African people, proverbs constitute a special language. Sometimes, for many, proverbs are considered both a secret and a sacred language in their communication where the expression—"talk in proverbial language" [zônzila mu bingana], an expression used within the community to prevent the leak of very fundamental principles of the society, i.e., to prevent the outsider from auditing the debate to have access to any basic systematic concepts of the structural organization of the society, especially it's secrecies. Once I was talking to an audience of more than thirty intellectuals and a friend of mine passed me, through the audience, a written word saying. "In such spots/places, talk superficially, don't dig at the bottom of things" [Ta mayulu-yulu mu bèndo bia mpila yâyi]. African people are very sensitive to what touches their conceptual bases.

Although African people enjoy talking in proverbial language, they also recognize that the use of this very philosophical language is dangerous, even mortal. Because of the danger presented by this language, one must understand perfectly the meaning of the proverb one uses because one kingana says "Wata ngana bângula ngana kadi Na Kimbônga-ngana wafwîla mu ngana"—literally, know the explanation of any proverb you use for sir "Proverb-teller" died upon the proverb he used. One may be condemned for what one says.

Proverbs, as a means of intellectual communication of great ideas within the community, are said and learned within the community, at a public house [ku mbôngi], in the market place, during the initiation period, during the work time, anywhere in the bush, on the street, at home as well as while running during a hunting party.

Proverbs, in African context, are laws, reflections, theories, customs, social norms and values, principles, and unwritten constitutions. They are used to justify what should be said or what has been said. Proverbs play a very important ethical role in storytelling, legends, etc. Very often parents as well as griots [n'samuni], and storytellers end their tales by very fitting proverbs.

African proverbs are numerous and diverse. They deal with people, God, ancestors, animals, forests, goods, money, ideas, wars, sun, moon, time, social problems, education, food, life, ku mpèmba (ancestor's world) traditions (kinkulu), history (kikulu), plants, insects, etc. We give here a short list of Kôngo proverbs, related to the community, in order to show our readers how rich these proverbs are, and perhaps they could reshape our corrupted young nations in Africa. Proverbs are laws [n'siku], principles [n'kîngu]. They define the African human rights [n'swa] as well.

It is my belief that African nations will not possibly be built upon outsider [fu] systems, as this proverb tells us "Kânda ka ditûngwanga va lwèka lwa fu kia nsi ko"—community is not built outside the social system of its inhabitants. The nation [nsi], like the community [kânda], must be built upon the national social system [fu-kia-nsi]. To build one's own society outside of one's own system is not only to weaken that society, but to destroy it. When a society is destroyed from its roots, one must expect all kinds of ailments that might accompany that destruction: disorganization, corruption, embezzlements, internal wars, insecurity, bankruptcy, violence, hostility against oneself, social injustice, poverty, famine, disease and death in masses.

Certain educated Africans pretend being more intelligent and more skilled than their uneducated ancestors. I don't know. Maybe it is so, but the same intellectuals forget what one says about those uneducated ancestors: Our ancestors did not have ***dictionaries*** or encyclopedias; true, but by their experiences, proverbs, and their sincere autocritiques, they did maintain and save the national and community security [Bakulu ka bavwa ***dîngu*** ko, i ngeta; kânsi mu nkuma, ngana ye ntungasani zâu zakedika balûnda luvuvamu lwa nsi ye kânda]. Could our intellectuals pretend to maintain that our communities' members are safe, secure, happy and well fed today? Maybe they do in their intellectual way, but I cannot say so. Besides, no generation in any society can claim superiority upon the former one. Learning and progress (civilization) are both building block processes. One does not exist without the other.

Regardless of our rejection of what we should really be, sooner or later, our nonsense intellectual realizations within our communities will be destroyed unless they are rooted on our social system [fu-kia-nsi], be they social, economical, political, philosophical, etc. The study of our languages may enable us to understand the systems, what they were, in case they were destroyed by the aggressor. Proverbs are one of the best ways that our concepts are well coded and thoroughly kept. Proverb study is a very rich and broad field that all African thought and wisdom lovers, linguists, philosophers, and all knowledge lovers should investigate. Proverbs for one main reason, in any African context, are regarded as the warehouse of the ancient African wisdom. They are very meaningful by themselves, and paramount in historical, philosophical, legal, religious and theoretical information about African schools of human knowledge. African youths and modern scholars must dig deeply for that knowledge if they wish to develop new theories about the development of modern Africa according to its realities. It is not a degradation to our young scholars if they do have some time to spend at our griots' feet to be "fed" by the past experience [nkuma], our cultural heritage [fwa dia lusânsu lwèto].

The young African "scholars" must agree that one's assimilated education is sometimes very meaningless within the context of African realities. Aware of this situation, it is advisable that one seeks, after one's studies abroad, contact with village sages to learn about their opinions for "The true leaders of opinion are not always the stereotyped well-educated, professional individuals active in official or voluntary work (M. Kochen, 1976:18)."

In a small area, Maniânga, in Lower-Congo, students of Luyalungunu lwa Kûmba-nsi Institute collected more than 1,500 proverbs and proper nouns in a short time. No one could convince those young people that African people did not have logical systems as it is always charged by certain biased groups. For them, thinkers such as Socrates, Plato, etc., existed only in the West. Africa did, as it does today, have its own "masters of thought" because their ideas remain with us: proverbs, legends, tales, myths, etc., even though their names are not known, because names are not very important in the African concept in the process of art creation. No one creates alone.

The proverbs below are excerpted from the unpublished *Dictionary of Nouns and Proverbs Kôngo*, [Dîngu kia Nkûmbu ye Ngana Zêto], collected under our direction (1964–73). This short list shows us how strong the concept of kânda (both a biological and social community) is among the Bântu people in particular and among African people in general.

The Kongolese word "kânda" has always been translated within western literature of Africa, in the anthropological point of view, as "clan", a word which has a negative connotation. This is not the way it is seen and understood by ourselves. As such, to be clear, the concept of community as it can be seen and understood in the African world does not exist in developed countries of the west. In those countries, from the African point of view, the word "community" is a meaningless word, empty of its meaning: Do you have any problem with foes, don't you believe it, if the police do not come as soon as possible, you may be killed on the street by that group and no one from your pretended community will dare to come out of his house to save your life. Their concept of law says so: "Don't involve yourself in somebody's elses affairs; that is his business." And this is the concept of law that the modern African is involved in, that is why our continent is swimming in blood.

Now let's examine these few proverbs, i.e., Kôngo thoughts related to the concept of "kânda", community; thoughts which are frequently repeated within the community about the community:

1) **Kânda mukûtu, variant Kânda mutu.**
The community/society did exist before you; the community leads everything, for it is the head. What is good for the community is good for its members. Everybody is a social product. One accepts the community as it is, not as one wants it to be.

2) **Kânda wakândula bièla bia kânda.**
The community massages its members' organs. The community solves community problems.

3) **Kânda wakânda mâmbu.**
The community leadership prevents problems and conflicts within the community. It is the responsibility of the community to create laws for its members.

4) **Vo zèyi kânda, zèyi Nzâmbi.**
If you know the community you know God. God is only visible through our attitude vis-a-vis our neighbors. Our existence creates God's existence.

5) **Nzâmbi mu kânda (kena).**
God (exists) in the community. The natural principle of change transmits itself perpetually in us through the community continuum.

6) **Untèla n'kîngu miankulu (mia kânda) kidi yazâya miampa, variant Wata diampa teka ta diankulu.**
Tell me the old principles/theories in order to understand the new ones. All educational process is gradual. Don't reverse the historical truth. History accumulates itself. One can only build on old materials. Natural laws are irreversible. To be born, one has first to be conceived. Before laughter there is funny hearing.

7) **Mbôngo a kânda ka mbôngo âku ko.**
The community's goods are not your goods. Public wealth is not private wealth. Don't put your hand upon public goods (wealth).

8) **Mu kânda, babo longa ye longwa.**
Within the community everybody has the right to

teach and to be taught. Education is a matter of reciprocity. True knowledge is acquired through sharing.

9) **N'kîngu mia kânda n'kîngu mia nsi.**
Principles (theories) of the community are also national principles. What belongs to the community belongs to the nation. What is private to a group is public to all groups. Individual productions contribute to community wealth.

10) **Kânda ka ditûngwanga va lwèka lwa fu kia nsi ko.**
The community, as well as the nation, is not built outside of its social system. A society is its concepts, be they political, philosophical, social or economical.

11) **Kânda n'landa: bankaka kwènda; bankaka kwîza,** ***variant***
Kânda ngongo: bankaka kwènda; bakaka kwîza.
The community is a channel: people go (die), people come (are born). The community renews perpetually its members and its principles accordingly to its [fu] systems, conforming to the natural laws, that of birth and death, the theory of [makwènda-makwîza], what goes will come back, the perpetual process of change through [dingo-dingo], the constant back and forth flow of [ngolo zanzîngila] living energy.

12) **Kutômbi didi dia minika mia kânda vo kwena mu kânda ko.**

Don't seek for the center of social waves if you don't belong within the community and its sytem. Do not force open somebody else's system's door when it is not open to you. The study of a system is possible only if it opens itself.

13) **Dia ye nwa, walambalala; bwatûngulwa bwâla kuzèyi bo ko.**
Eat, drink, and then sleep for you ignore how the village was built. Just watch and see, don't be involved in fundamental social issues of cultural and systematic discrepancies.

14) **Kutômbi didi dia (ngolo za) zûnga ko kwidi zûngwa (cfrl 2).**
Don't seek to know the regional center of driving forces for fear of being confined by these forces.

15) **Sîmbi bia nsi (bia kânda) mu kilômbo binikukinanga.**
Societal leaders move and act through masses. A true leader mingles in the crowd. A leader that stands aloof to his people is a puppet.

16) **Kânda diakuta Nzûndu, nkio[5] diawunuka, ukitèle Zûndu. Nga zêyi diswasâni diena va kati kwa Nzûndu ye Zûndu e ?**
The community named you Nzûndu,[6] you thought

---

5. Nkio', shortening of nkiôngono.

6. Nzûndu; anvil—symbol of productivity within the community. Name given to a child wherein the community hopes that his birth will revive its stagnant economy.

it was mistaken itself; you call yourself Zûndu[7]. Can you tell the existing difference between Nzûndu and Zûndu?

This proverb contains a very simple, but basic philosophical truth about proper noun meaning among the African people, the self, i.e., a) to be what one is, and b) to try to realize what the community (society) expects from you in accordance to the label (name) you bear. If the community wants you to be "Community-Anvil" [Nzûndu-a-kânda], be that community "Anvil" and don't make yourself a "Frog-Within-The-Community" [zûndu-mu-kânda], i.e. a "Drunkard-Within-The-Community." (For more information read our Makuku Matatu, Chapter 2).

17) **Nga nzènza mûntu katûnga fu kia bwâla?**
Could a strange person build a favorable social system of a village that is not his own? Community members only, of a given society, are able to do what a stranger cannot do for its safety as well as for its human well-being. No one can do better for you than yourself.

[7]. Zûndu; by fault of eliminating the "N" from the above name, the name becomes Zûndu (frog); for the Kôngo, Zûndu is the symbol of drunkard, but also of habitual drunkeness. In suppressing certain letters, mainly "n" and "m" from their names, many intellectuals in present Africa bear names with a vulgar meaning or simply meaningless names, as in the case of the name Zûndu.

18) **Wampâna nsèngo, kunkâmbi kwè ngâtu bwè isadila yo ko.**
If you give me a hoe don't tell me where or how I should use it. Don't stifle my field of activities and my normal development by pretended assistance.

19) **Kânda diazûngulwa lusunga lwa kimfumu-dikânda luzîmbale.**
When the community leadership looses its direction, the community is oppressed. There is only the leadership and its direction that should be blamed in any social, economic or political crises. One spits only at the leader.

20) **Ka ngw'ândi ko, kânda dian'kitula kinsevanseva ye luntoyo.**
It is the community that made him/her a habitual smiler and a talkative individual, not his/her mother. Community members are born simple, nice, and good, but they become what the community wants them to be/become. The human being is a social product; he is what he eats, learns, hears, sees, feels, and lives. The actual behavior of a human being is a learned behavior. Very often one's nature is oppressed by the society.

21) **Kânda kându: ka kilôswa; ka kisâmbu.**
The community is a taboo: never can one throw it away, and never can one worship it. No one can be otherwise than what one is. Societies, like human beings, have their own identities/ personalities, be they open or hidden.

22) **Kânda diansânsa, kânda isânsa.**
The community took care of me; I will take care of that community. Community life is a process of receiving and transmitting/passing on. [tâmbula ye tambikisa] Teach a child completely and thoroughly about what you are as a community and your teaching will go on completely and thoroughly. Life and living is a seedling process.

23) **Kiasôla kânda ko; kânda diansôla.**
I did not choose my community (society/race); it is the community that chose me by giving birth to me/by bringing me where I am. The community has responsibilities to me as I have responsibilities vis-a-vis to it. Discrimination is a disease.

24) **Kânda diasâla nsâng'a n'kènto ka ditûmbukanga ko.**
As long as there is a female "shoot" within the community, it cannot be annihilated. The presence of a female in the community is the symbol of continuity of life in that community, and on the contrary, her absence is the symbol of its end. The feminine is life (God) in and around us.

25) **Kânda diamôyo dîmbu yèmba.**
The common and public house is the symbol of an alive community. The yèmba/boko is the point of centralization and decentralization of forces as well as of activities within the community. Its animation is a sign of vitality within the community. Well seated institutions are key to social, economical, political, and philosophical stability of

nations; they are, not only nations' hearts, but also their brains.

26) **Kânda nkasa ye nome/niosi.**
The community is at the same time poison and honey. The community is very sticky to its members. It is hard, even hostile to live within, but it is however the best place to "stick on" [nama], i.e., to live and to belong to.

27) **Kânda i (mbûndani a) bafwa ye bamôyo.**
The community is the union of the ancestors and of the living people. The community is an accumulation of the living unity of the physical and spiritual elements.

28) **Mu kânda ka mwena nzaku (za n'toto) ko.**
There are no boundaries of land within the community land. The freedom of land use by all community members is warranted within the community. There is no privacy on land issues; its ownership is public for no one came in this world with a piece of land in his/her hand. Therefore it cannot be sold, bought or alienated.

29) **Wasînga kânda ukisîngidi.**
If you curse the community you curse yourself. It is uneasy for one to blame or condemn one's community. Avoid the attack of the community against you.

30) **Wakatuka mu n'kîngu mia fu kia kânda kitukidi mapeka ye wûngani.**

If you do leave the principles of the community system, you become an errant and a deviant. The loss of one's own rights of belonging to a community (society/nation) is maybe more harmful than an imprisonment for life.

31) **Kânda diafûka nza yifûkidi.**
If the concept of community is annihilated/ destroyed, the world is destroyed. If principles, concepts, norms and values that make world communities alive are violated, weakened or completely destroyed, the human being will easily destroy his world.

32) **Yimbu mu kânda sînsu kia mfwîlu a kânda.**
The poison within the community is a symptom of community/social destruction. Deadly weapons in man's community not only are a symbol of the disorganization of the society which possess them, but more importantly they are a symptom of its own destruction, and of the approaching end of man's world.

33) **Dièla dia kânda m'bikudi.**
The wisdom of the community prophesizes. The community sees farther than an individual can. Anyone who learns to see through the community's eyes (wisdom) is a very bright person.

34) **Kala n'lôngi a kânda mbo' wazâya mayenda mu kânda.**

Be a community teacher/leader in order to know what goes on within the community. The real wisdom of a society and its very basic needs are only known by those who mingle within the reality of people's daily lives in that society.

35) **Kânda kabelanga nzènza ko.**
The community is not hostile to a stranger. The community welcomes all human beings as long as they do not dare to interfere with its basic social practices/principles.

36) **Kubungi kûmu kia kânda mu kinzènza kiâku ko.**
Do not try to destroy the reputation of the community/society while wearing, somewhere else, the label of "being a stranger." Your misconduct, elsewhere, has direct or indirect impact on your community/society as well as on yourself.

37) **Mvita makânda mawûbi ulèndanga zo.**
The quarrels (wars) between communities/societies are solved by diplomatic encounters. The diplomacy [kimawûbi] is the leading key to peace.

38) **Ku kânda dia mbadio mpaka (ntantani) ze' ko; nga ziswèmi mu dia diâku zazèyi?**
There are lots of conflicts within the "So's" community; do you realize how many there are within yours? Tend to your affairs and let others preoccupy themselves with theirs. Try to learn thoroughly what is going on in your own society before probing other societies.

39) **Lumbu-ki bisikânda, mbazi bakulu ba kânda, variant Lumbu-ki lesi bia kânda, mbazi bakulu mu kânda.**
Today we are community members; tomorrow we will be the ancestors of the community. What we do and think today prepares us for what will be the community's assessment tomorrow. If we are today, simple individuals within the community, we may tomorrow be deified (spiritualized), i.e. be considered as the source of driving forces and radiations within the living community, and this in accordance with our attitude vis-a-vis to that community during our physical lifetime [ku nseke]. Any seed can give life to a big tree.

40) **Mu kânda kikânda, bukânda, kinkwèzi, kimwânambuta, kisikânda, kikûndi, kinzâyani. Ka mwena kimpala ko.**
Within the community there are all alliances:community righteousness, marriage alliances, affiliation, friendship, relationship; there is no antagonism. It is pleasant to live within a community, for in the community, in the African concept, indeed your pain and pleasure are shared, your joys doubled, even tripled. The community, your community as well as my community, is your place of joy, love and life.

41) **Mwîsi wa mbôngi a kânda wubote ke lusekeseke lwa nim'a lônde ko.**
Better the smoke from the community's public house rather than warmth from beyond our bound-

aries. Social conflicts within the community are less harmful than an exile.

42) **Kânda diakôndwa n'toto, bilesi bilaukidi/bimwângane.**
If the community lacks the land, the door for survival, its members will disperse. The community land, its availability to all members, is the symbol of security and of togetherness within the community. A community leader as well as a national one must know that community/national land is the first property of the society that should be protected, even at the price of blood. A leader that sells or alienates the land of the community/society is a murderer, because he prevents the community/society from having access to its first source of all possibilities for survival.

43) **Dûnga mu kânda ka (biena) kinkuma ko.**
Events within the community are not a rarity. Human community always has problems to confront. Life within the community is a perpetual debate. To be a community member is to be ready to confront problems.

44) **N'samu mia kânda miale' bulungi, variant N'samu mia kânda ka mivwîdi bulungi ko: mia ndo ka ndo.**
Community issues (affairs) do not have anniversaries; they happen anytime. Anything at anytime may happen within the community. With regard to anniversaries, they belong to seasons, plants, and to living beings. Any community member as well as any

community leader must be aware about the "kôndwa-kwa-bulungi" principle in community affairs.

45) **Wazangisa Kimvwâma zîmbisi n'swa ye niènzi mu kânda.**
In worshipping one's own wealth one looses rights and social enjoyment of his/her community. Mûntu, the human being, is fundamentally a social being and, as such, his assumed private rights are very meaningless before the social and collective rights. A shared wealth procures more internal happiness.

46) **Makani ma kânda, mwâna mu ntûnda; ka mate-wanga nkûmbu ko.**
Community plans/projects, are an infant in their mother's womb, they are without name. Social driving forces, their sources, are fundamentally unknown. If the name of your plan/project explicitly tells you what you want to do, don't tell it to your enemy, and the best way to keep it secret is to knot it = code it [kânga yo kolo].

47) **Kolo diakânga ngânga, kutula ngânga, variant Kolo diakanga mwisikânda, mwisikânda kutula dio or Kolo diakânga mwisikânda, kutula mwisikânda.**
A code (knot) from a specialist should be decoded by a specialist (of the system=kimpa, fu). What is fundamentally systematic can only be easily understood within the system. Our present knowledge in ways of coding and decoding cultural codes of alien cultures is the cornerstone in human antagonism in the world today.

48) **Mfumu-dikânda n'tu a mbwa watôndila makome.**
The community leader is a dog's head; everybody knocks upon it. One only spits at the leader. A true leader is an object of critics.

49) **Kwena sîmbi kia kânda, kwena didi dia kânda.**
Where there is the community djinn (leadership), there is the center of the community. Societies like people have their hearts.

50) **Kisikânda, vo ka butukila ko (mu) bukwângi.**
If not by birth, one becomes a member of the community by refuge (adoption/exile). All means are available to integrate a society.

51) **Kânda, kându kia kânda ye nsi.**
The community is a taboo for the community and for the nation. National pride is made by men of deeds, members of national communities. There are not two different laws in one nation: one for the poor and the other for the rich or one for the village and another for the city.

52) **Bându dia kânda nsâng'a mûntu ye n'toto.**
The initial community capital (bându, from bânda, to start) is its human resources and the land. Life would be impossible within the community without land and without valid people in it. The community must pay a particular attention to its youth as well as to its land, the fundamental capitals of a society.

53) **Mbôngi nkat'a kânda ye nsi.**

The public house of the community is the seating of the community as well as of the nation. Community unity finds its foundation from "boko", the public house/institution. Societies as well as people, have their rolls of life; these rolls, nzingu/nkata, are rolled and unrolled within social and public institutions.

54) **Mbûngi a kânda va kati kwa nsi ye yulu.**
The center (cavity) of the community is located between the above and below world. The reality of the cultural heritage of a community, i.e., its knowledge, is the experience of that deepest knowledge found between the spiritualized ancestors and the physically living thinkers within the community.

Africa was invaded in all its regions by travellers, missionaries, newsmen, pilots, peacemakers, apartheid-minded-individuals, and today, by "bought-men", the mercenaries, with the main goal, in accordance to what one tells us, to understand and to civilize its people. The mission of civilization having "accomplished" her "noble" mission, which was a total failure, African people were still known as people without logic, people without systems, people without concepts, the primitive people, unlawful societies, etc. And one may ask what is wrong with social science scholars and their academic world? How long should we continue to lie? Proverbs related to the community, and our comments on them prove the contrary of what has always been said and taught about African people. They tell us how lawful, philosophical, systematic and practical

African people were in their own world. Should not one be astonished by African wisdom, should one undertake a more or less complete study of that African wisdom hidden in proverbs, the old way of theorizing among people of oral literature? One must understand that a proverb, for African people and those with a basically oral literature, is not seen and understood in the way the western world sees and understands it. For us, because of the lack of material to write on in the past, proverbs are principles, theories, warehouses of knowledge, booklets, taped information, and, above all, they have "force de loi", force of law, in judiciary circumstances. A court without *proverbs* (translated here as judiciary referential legal documents) belongs to the dead [Mbasi-a-n'kanu yakôndwa bingana ya bafwa], says an unwritten Kôngo constitutional legal passage/proverb.

Hearing Is Seeing, and Seing Is Reacting/Feeling

Wa i mona, ye mona i sunsumuka

Life is fundamentally a process of perpetual and mutual communication; and to communicate is to emit and to receive waves and radiations [minika ye minienie]. This process of, receiving and releasing or passing on [tâmbula ye tambikisa] is the key to human being's game of survival. A person is perpertually bathed by radiations' weight, [zitu kia minienie]. The weight [zitu/demo] of radiations may have a negative as well as a positive impact on any tiny being, for example a person who represents the most vibrating "kolo" (knot) of relationships. The following expressions are very common among the Bântu, in general, and among the Kôngo, in particular, which prove to us the antiquity of these concepts in the African continent; Our businesses are waved/shaken; our health is waved/shaken; what we possess is waved/shaken; the communities are waved/shaken: Where are these (negative) waves coming from [Salu bièto bieti nikunwa; mavîmpi nikunwa; bituvwîdi nikunwa; makânda nikunwa: Kwè kutûkanga minika miâmi]?

For the Bântu, a person lives and moves within an ocean of waves/radiations. One is sensitive or immune to them. To be sensitive to waves is to be able to react negatively or positively to those waves/forces. But to be immune to surrounding waves/forces, is to be less reactive to them or not at all. These differences account for varying degrees in the process of knowing/learning among individuals.

A sickness may be caused by waves/radiations sent or emitted by a strange body within a given milieu. Although the subject has already been discussed otherwise in Kindoki and Makuku Matatu, we repeat this discussion here to help those who may not have the chance to read my previous works. The following picture will be very helpful.

When a vibrating knot [kolo] of relationships, i.e. a living being M, is in communication with a visible source of waves, VSW, in a radius [n'nienie] of audibility AB on the line of the waves' extent direction, AC, one knows that little or no attention is paid to the importance of the waves/vibrations. Images and voice/sound alone are the important factors of this communication. On the other hand, images and voices/sounds alone can disturb such a communication. Remark that the intensity of the voice/sound [zu/n'nîngu] diminishes as one becomes oblivious to all directions (upwards, downwards, backwards, or sideways) from VSW. If the voice from VSW cannot be heard outside the circle of audibility [lukôngolo lwangwîla] formed by the radius AB, we then say that the point B is the point where the "voiced-wave-message" becomes a voiceless-waved-message". Beyond this point voices become less important, i.e., waves/vibrations and images invade the B-C field of communication.

These waves and images can be disturbed by other waves and images. This disturbance, like what happened to the disturbed voices, may confuse the original message. This is why it is very often difficult for the invisible destination ID, e.g., the dreamer, located in any point in the field of communication BC within waves' strata [nyalu/ngwèngwe a minika], 7-0, to understand the communication.

In a crowded place, it is easy for someone to be confused about one's own name when called by someone else standing at VSW. This may happen because of the existence of other voices/forces are the disturbing agents throughout the field of communication A-B in its diverse points of waves' strata [ngwèngwe za minika] 13-8. One has to be told by somebody else that "you are called." This teller [sunsumuni/te] was able to hear the calling voice/vibrations from the VSW, because he was more aware and more sensitive to that voice hearing is seeing, and seeing is reacting/feeling [Wa i mona, ye mona i sunsumuka]. There is a fundamental relationship between hearing, seeing and feeling/reacting [wa, mona ye sunsumuka]. Feeling is understanding. The Bântu do not "feel" pain, unless they "see" them [mona mpasi] as we have said in our second chapter. To have one's senses in a perfect state of health is to have the key to the basic process of accumulating knowledge. One who does not have one's senses in that state is said to be, at a certain level, a mentally "disabled" person, i.e., a being scored under the level of knowing [tûlwa/kiâtwa ku nsia tèzo kia zâya/nzailu].

What was said above reveals the pattern in the process of natural voiceless communications throughout, waves/radiations and dreams [minika/miniemie ye ndozi] as we discussed the issue in Makuku Matatu.

A dream [ndozi] is a voiceless communication. It is at the same time a means and a message. This message can be audible, pictorial and scenic. It has an origin [tûku], a channel [ngongo/n'landa], with or without an addressee receptor [tâmbudi]. The origin/source of the message can be natural, spiritual or supernatural. Before becoming a dream [ndozi], this communication was a "wireless" communication from its source (say the point VSW within the waves' strata 13), to the point at which it becomes a dream (i.e., any point within the field of communication B-C). Such a communication is voiceless from any point outside of the wave stratum circle B through the field of communication B-C to the wave stratum circle C. Certain waved communications are voiceless from their origin, say VSW, to C, i.e., to the endless [sènsele]. The communication passes through two main fields A-B and B-C, before becoming a dream at the point where the dreamer stands, say at the point C.

In the first field, A-B, this communication was principally a "voiced-pictorial-waved-message" [n'samu-wangwa-wambona-wanikunwa]. In this same field, other positive or negative "voiced-pictorial-waved-messages" are able to disturb the first one. These disturbing messages, i.e., the unwanted ones, can be under diverse forms: noise, call, event, scream, picture, a motion/movement, a laugh, etc.

On the contrary, in the second field, B-C, the communication becomes principally a "vibrated-pictorial-voiceless-message" [n'samu-wanikunwa-wambona-wadikama]. While running through this field, the waved message can also be disturbed by other waved and unwanted messages. In other words, this message becomes entangled with all kinds of symbols and images, and is said to be "sticky" [n'samu weka lunama]. These sticky and unwanted messages add to the true and original message/communication different symbolic forms which are very often bizarre and frightening: sinking in water or in volcanic lava; burying oneself; lizards, being surrounded by red-hot-lava, and all kinds of nightmares. These symbolic images cover deeply and entirely the true meaning of the dream. One then has to undergo the process of removing or of discarding all those false symbols and their unwanted meanings added to the dream's message in order to discover the true symbol of that dream and its meaning to the dreamer or to his community. This elimination process is to dig up the garbage or rubbish [sâta mfuti].

Because the dreamer cannot always understand the message contained in his dream, he needs help just as in the case of the person who could not hear the call of his name only with the aid of an intermediary who was sensitive enough to understand the call. In the case of the process of explaining dreams, this helper is called dream-interpreter [m'bângudi-a-ndozi]. The dream can be a reflection of diurnal activities, a repetition of past activities, or a projection of one's own activities and imagination in the future. But, most importantly, it can be a warning about a future or imminent event: good or bad news. A dream-interpreter [M'bângudi-a-ndozi], is a person whose sensitivity to and awareness of waves, symbols and their meanings are very high. There is a lot to learn through the dream state [ndozi], about people and their health, about societies and their organizations, about science, the past, the present and the future of humanity and the world. But only a few people can understand them. The scholar as well as the common man, very often, are unable to see what is true or false in a dream, the waved-sticky-message [n'samu-wa-lunama-wanikunwa].

The Bântu/Kôngo concept of dream [ndozi], is the direct application of their theory about radiation. This theory is very popular in African daily expressions, but ignored by African intellectuals as well as by African wisdom lovers. In accordance with this theory [lôngi diâdi], it is the waves/radiations that shake/wave societies, nations and communities [i minika/minienie minikunânga bimvuka, zinsi ye makânda]. In other words, it is the waves/radiations [minika/minienie], which are very often the cause of accidents, sicknesses, fatigue, tensions, changes, etc., (see Kindoki). Radiations of a strange body within a given milieu, as well as words, may have a catastrophic impact upon that environment.

It is 1939. I was 5 years old. A man of the true name Matidi-Mukôdia, in the village of Kûmbi, came into the picture (était à la page). This man, after the loss of many of his family members, underwent a psychological crisis. Without the knowledge of the other inhabitants of the village, he went to buy strong baneful "knots" (sachets) of an n'kisi [mafutu ma n'kisi wambi] and he interred them, at night, throughout the entire village and in all its exits [mafula]. Three weeks after this undercover operation the entire village was shaken/waved by strange ailments [vata diadio dianikunwa kwa mpila vûnga bianzènza] People screamed and murmured: where are these waves coming from that shake/wave the village? [Bântu bakwâya ye vunguta: Kwè kweti tûkanga minika mieti nikuna vata?]

Because of this social imbalance, locale elders called for an urgent debate/meeting in order to "nail/hammer the issue" and "knot it" in nkôndi, the "problem-nailing-recorder-object," [sîmbi bia vata biavwândisa bântu mu koma binko ye kânga/loka nkôndi/mfûna] i.e., send defensive waves/radiations through the village via the air and the earth in order to "attack" the source of those negative radiations and the wrong-doer at their center (See figure 21).

A few days after the ritual ceremony of tying the "vibrating knot" of social self-defense, Matidi-Mukôdia lost his equilibrium and became seriously sick. The village council sat again to discuss the issue and interview the dying sickman. Matidi accepted his guilt and explained what he did. It was a Sunday. Matidi-Mukôdia asked the crowd to follow him in order to unearth all the negative vibrating knots [mafutu/makolo ma minika miambi] he had interred in the village, which were the source of the negative waves [minika miambi] that shook the whole village. We all went after him to see, with our own eyes, the n'kisi that waved/shook the community of the village. After the operation had been unearthed the negative waves disappeared from the village [minika miambi miavila mu vata].

Superstition? Hallucination? Magic manipulation? Unscientific-related issue? I cannot tell. One sole thing I know, it happened and I was among the witnesses on the spot.

When a Mûntu, in general, and a Mukôngo, in particular, says our bodies are being shaken/waved [nitu zèto zeti nikunwa bèni] or our community is being ghastly shaken/waved again and again [kânda dièto dieti nikunwa ye nikunwa] or we are in a waving/vibrating period [mu tându kia ndikununu/ndikutusunu twena], he is referring to that theory of waves/radiations which can positively or negatively bathe and shake/wave bodies, nations, governments and communities/socieities, be they developing or advanced. Likewise when a, deep-going person, psychiatrist, seer [m'fièdi/ngûnza], says people are murmuring about you [bântu beti kwènda niungutanga mu ngeye] or you are followed by bad luck [n'loko weti kulândanga], he is referring to that theory [lôngi]. These waves may have good or bad consequences upon people, nations and social organizations [Minika miâmi milènda tûkisa lèmina diambi evo diambote mu bântu, zinsi ye mu bimvuka]. Three cases are meanwhile possible in this process of communication by natural or supernatural waves/radiations:

1. The human being, receiver [tâmbudi], i.e., dreamer, can receive and understand thoroughly the waved

message [n'samu wanikunwa/tubwa] and take then his precautions. The receptibility, like the audibility, depends not only on the perfectibility (health) and sensibility of the senses, but also on the distance and obstacles met in the field of communication [yînza dia ntambukusulu/dia minika].

2. He can only receive and understand a part of the waved message, whereby a certain anxiety and doubt comes to the dreamer/receiver in accordance with what I dreamed, I doubt if people in my village community are fine [Kizèyi ko keti ku vata mbote kwâu bena].

3. He may not receive the message at all. In this case he is totally ignorant of it, whereupon baneful, disastrous and unforeseen consequences may affect his daily life.

Because of this, the Mûntu will, for a dream, consult the m'fièdi, deep-heart-going-person, dream-interpreter [m'bângudi-a-ndozi], soothsayer [m'moni-a-mâmbu], seer-through-life-rolls [n'zingumuni-a-mâmbu]. He may also decide to discuss the situation in a community council, with a wise friend, or if such be the case, "kângisa mio, i.e., minika", literally tie/knot them, i.e., code them into a vibrating knot that could produce defensive radiations/waves in order to avoid undesirable or disastrous consequences within the community.

It is using both mental and natural laser power [Lèndo kiampîtila]. And man continues to dream old as well as new dreams in the same way his great-great-great-grandparents dreamt.

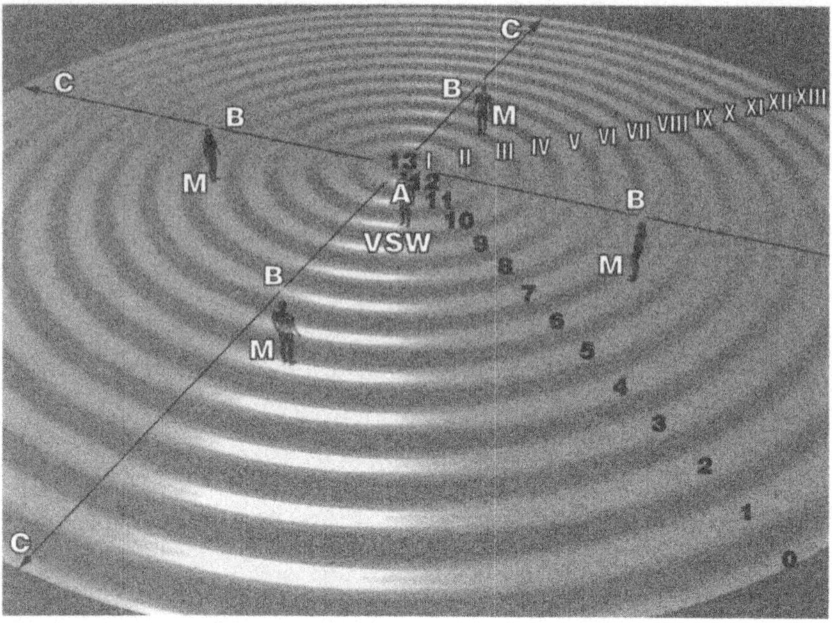

Figure 21.

A: *Center/source of emission [didi/nto a ntubulu/ndikusunu]*
B: *Radius' end of field of audibility [nsuk'a n'nienie wa yînza dia ngwîlu]*
BC: *Endless field of the reception of voiceless waves [sènsele/ yînza diakôndwa nsuka dia ntambudulu a minika miadingalala]*
M: *Receptor of voiced/audible message [tâmbudi kia n'samu wawâkana]*
AC: *Line direction of waves' extent [n'lông'a lusunga lwa mbwangununu a minika*
VSW: *Visible source of waves. Human being's voice in circle A [Tûku kia-monika kia Minika, TAM- Zu dia mûntu mu kindiongololo A].*
I-XIII: *Roman figures indicate different distances in the fields of reception. Figure I indicates the shortest distance from the VSW, and XIII indicates the longest distance. [Sono bia Lôma bieti sônga nswâsani a tatuka kwenamu bèndo bia ntambudulu. Dîmbu I kieti sônga tini kilutidi nkufi ye kilutidi finama ye TAM (VSW) ye dîmbu XIII, tini kilutidi nda ye kilutidi tatuka ye TAM].*
13-0: *Arabic figures indicate frequencies of waves emitted, their amount. The figure O indicates the field of communication as yet untouched by emitted waves. The figure 1 indicates the first layer of waves emitted by the VSW, and the number 13 the last layer of waves sent from VSW [Sono bia kialabia bieti songa ndikit'a minika mitubulu, ntalu âu. Dîmbu O kieti sônga yînza dilèmbolo lwâkwa kwa minika mitubulu. Dîmbu 1 kieti sônga nyalu yantete ya minika mitubulu kwa TAM ye, ntalu/nomba 13 yeti sônga nyalu yaz-imunina/yansuka ya minika mitubulu kwa TAM].*

Is That Magic?

Ket'i Muyeke?

When one fundamentally understands an African language and the symbolic cultural concepts generated by that language, one must wonder where technological direction the African traditional concept of knowing [zâya] is heading. Can we today, with our present system of coding and decoding cultural concepts, be able to unearth that yet unknown dimension?

Lèmba-dia-Kânda, literally "The Soother-of-the-Community", was the unique sister of Baniunguta-Kwâu, literally "Let-Them-Murmur", and the unique sister of the community [kânda]. Unexpectedly Lèmba-dia-Kânda was kidnapped on her way to the field. She was badly beaten and left for dead by her unknown kidnapper. The community in its entirety was shocked by this unhuman treatment.

Baniunguta-Kwâu, Lèmba-dia-Kanda's brother, took the initiative to see, the specialist-owner of the televisor-pot [ngânga-sènso] in order to get revenge on his sister. "The initiative is positive," agreed the whole community.

"We want to know who the kidnapper was of the community's unique sister," the only question asked of the ngânga-sènso. You will, right now, see the proof about the kidnapper of the unique community sister," [Si lwamona kimansuna] responded the ngânga. The ngânga put his sènso in the middle of the circle; he then put in some clear water and medicines [maza malônga ye bikôla]. He asked the elder of the community and the kidnapped sister to wash their hands within the sènso, the televisor-pot[8].

After this ritual, the ngânga-sènso covered his sènso with a piece of red cloth. He then talked to himself in a very strange language and, pointing to the elder of the community said uncover "the televisor-pot" [Yabula sènso]. Surprisingly, everybody could see the unknown kidnapper within the plate (pot) beating the unique community sister. "What do you want?" [Bwâbu nki luzolele], said the ngânga "Do what you usually do" [Sa bu usânga], "Break the needle; kill him" [tabula ntûmbu] responded the community members.

The ngânga took the knife appropriated for the practice and knocked it on the head of the kidnapper whose shadow was radiating within the sènso. At once the clear water was transformed (changed) into blood., the enemy of the community is unmistakably hit [N'tântu wa kânda utèlo].

Is that magic [ket'i muyeke] or just unthinkable discourses of the so called "primitive" and "illogical" people by

8. Sènsa: To appear (from far away), coming to visibility, to approach, to reveal itself.
Sènsinsa: To make appear or visible, to bring to visibility, to make closer, to develop (picture).
Sènsisi: The one that manipulates or uses the sènso/sensosolo. Developer (photo).
Sènso: Appearance, visibility, screen, televisor-pot, movie, television set.
Sensosolo: Instrument and product to make appear (photo), binoculars. Synonym of sènso.

the specialists of the understanding of man? Or a precursor of the yet unknown field whose ground is already laid in Africa? This is one of the "knowing" aspects aborted by colonization everywhere in the world.

The African concept of knowing [zâya], about waves [minika], still is fundamentally unearthed; it does have a different direction within a different dimension; maybe it is unfelt because it is unknown by specialists of the current well known concept of knowing/knowledge [zâya/nzailu].

Figure 22.

If a Mukôngo, in particular, and a Mûntu in general, sits down for awhile on one side of his/her path, he will make sure before leaving that he picked up [bônga bèndo] his electronic radiated shadow [kîni kia minika/minienie kisîdi va bèndo] left on the spot where he was sitting: To pick up one's own radiated shadow left on the seated spot [bônga bèndo/kîni, variant bônga kîni kia minienie mia bèndo], for fear of being manipulated by one's own enemy in case this enemy possesses delicate knowledge about [kîni kia bèndo], the electronically radiated shadow (sensibility) upon things we touch or sit down on.

Do not such concepts reflect a high level of thinking about electronics and advanced concepts in technology? Are not concepts and ideas, be they mythical, utopian or magic, precede all inventions? Would our present world's main concept of knowing [zâya] change when this concept fully comes to its visibility or understanding [mbwèno yâyi bu yina sènsa va mpènza]? I cannot tell because I don't know, but one thing is true people will be curious about it. Then we will see if this concept will not stop, for the sake of world peace, the appearance of the world's unwanted leaders' faces from the TV screen [sènso] because of their undemocratic, dictatorial and "mandateless" regimes.

Figure 23.

IV

The "V": Basis of All Realities

In 1964, at the age of 30, I was introduced to one of the most important, secret, and sacred teaching of Kôngo; a Bântu speaking ethnic group in the center of West Africa, along the shores of the Atlantic Ocean. Here the word Bantu should be understood as an anthropological term. As such, one has to see and understand it as a complex house with tens, if not hundreds or rooms. Each of these rooms will be seen, understood, and taken as an ethnic group such as that of the Kôngo people.

These teachings of Kôngo were offered at the Lèmba Institute in Maniânga, the Lower-Congo where I was born. This institute was one of five main institutes that existed in the ancient Kôngo kingdom prior to the Colonial Era. The four others were Kimpasi, Kinkîmba, Bwèlo and Kikûmbi. The last, Kikûmbi Institute, was specialized to focus on womanhood and all its related issues. All teachings in these institutes were Bântu people teachings, i.e., related to the complexity of the "Bântu house" as they were disseminated within "Kôngo room."

Because of their secrecy, sacredness, as well as their mystic nature, only initiated individuals were allowed to enter these institutions. The exception is Kikûmbi that requires one major condition for any female candidate to enter: The condition to enter the womanhood institution is to "be of age." This means to have had one's first menstruation [yikama or kala ku mbôngo]. It is at this stage that a female candidate of Bântu culture in the Kôngo area is introduced to the secrecy and sacredness of the first "V", in both its biological aspects to life and living in the "inner environment" of any life to be [Fu-Kiau, 1991]. The Kîkumbi was the only institution that disseminated not only the secrecy and sacredness of the first "V" to its candidtaes, but its mystic meaning as well!

To illustrate to these candidates that the teachings were highly powerful, secret and sacred, all candidates were painted with the tukula (red), the symbol of both danger and death, maturity and leadership. The symbolic painting of candidates in red [tukula] was fundamental to convey the essence of the teaching to all. This prevented these teachings from being violated by those who offer the first environment, the inner environment, to any living being to be born. Here we are talking about what I call the reverse "Vee", as it will be discussed.

Because of their closed door policy to the non-initiated [biyînga], colonial powers decreed these institutions as dangerous to the survival of colonization. Consequently, these institutions were destroyed without taking into consideration their social, cultural, educational, spiritual or moral values. Many of their unyielding leading masters [ngudia-ngânga] were executed or jailed for life. The remaining masters took these institutions underground for hundreds of years for fear of reprisal from both the colonial and religious powers.

It is at the feet of some of these underground masters that I learned not only about the "V" (the basis of all realities), but the foundation of the Bântu people system of thought as well, their cosmologies. No one can truly understand the "Vee" without any basic knowledge upon Bântu world view, or their cosmologies. Our own work, as would later write two American scholars, is the first on the subject: "This study is the first in any language to reveal the system of popular Kôngo religion, its cosmology" [McGaffey et. al. 1974].

Understanding the world view of a people is the cornerstone for understanding their culture. If the Bântu cosmology was only revealed to the outside world by 1966, a few years after the liberation of most Bântu people area, then one can also say that the Bântu world is yet not truly understood by the outside world—neither culturally, artistically, nor philosophically. Therefore, western literature of Africa prior to this date must contain many fantasies which must be dismissed if one is willing to contribute to the process of "Building African scholarship in Africa and Diaspora."[1] Superficial scholarship anywhere in the world is very dangerous in terms of human relationships. It is always better to remain quiet than to utter wrong statements about other cultures (come to haunt you). Many of the world's tensions today are the results of such wrong statements.

---

1. Fu-Kiau, 1997: Title of a lecture given at Iowa State University.

It is not easy for outsiders to access the cultural core of a given people unless one is guided by a local native master. This is the case of the "Vee" here. This Kôngo "V" was never talked or written about because it is an integral part of the Kôngo cosmology; a world view that was never revealed before 1966 by local masters. Now we are able to talk about and discuss it openly as it was understood and disseminated in ancient institutions of the Bântu world.

The "Vee", what is it? One may promptly ask.

Because this subject is exciting and vital to life, I have lectured on this subject many times since I have been living in the States; both privately and publicly, in colleges, universities, museums, cultural centers, and in jails as well. Everything, including individual and collective life depends upon it. National security itself, of any country, is subject to it. And yet, it remains a secret to the great majority because they are not aware of it. The "V" is one of the most important keys in understanding life on the planet earth, and in the cosmic bodies (planets) as well (if life exists there too). It is, in some way, life itself (as we "try" to know it). Everything is a "V" because the beginning itself, or the big bang, exploded in the form of the "V". Because it is the bridging "wire" between thinking-matter the human [mûntu], and the world of unthinking-matter (the world and source of "ungrasped" ideas and images). The "Vee" is the basis of all inspirational realities such as great ideas, images, illustrations, inventions of all orders (including works of art), wars and conceptions, both biological and ideological as well. It is the process [dingo-dingo] to all changes, social and institutional; natural and unnatural, seen and unseen.

To talk about the "V" is to talk about realities, whether they are biological, inspirational or ideological, material or immaterial. They all pop into our minds in forms of the Vee (beam span of the Vee) inside us at the Musoni zone of the Kôngo cosmology. We seek for ideas and images through "the open beam of the Vee" inside our mind and on the contrary we focus details and specificities under reverse beam of the "Vee". This "V" is not a religion nor an academic exercise which may consist of transferring bones from one graveyard to another. It is one of the most secret keys of life and living.

Cosmically, the Vee teaches with all simplicity the formation process [dingo-dingo] of the universe and its bodies or planets [Fu-Kiau, 1994] while biologically, it explains the formation as well as the developmental process of life through all its stages; conception, birth, maturity, and death. With the Vee one can ideologically understand social systems: their rise and their fall (Fu-Kiau, 1980).

The "Vee" has a standing ground, the untouchable "dark matter" that consitutes the "printing dark room" of realities. From this dark room, pictures and ideas become realities in human minds which channel them into transformation processes that lead them to tangible realities. "Vee" is the core to all circles inside which "Vee" stands. These "Vees" are individual or collective, material or immaterial, biological or ideological. Inside the community circle's "Vee" stands the master [ngânga], teacher, priest, as a power figure. This power figure, the leader/priest [ngânga], who stands powerfully at the center of the community issues [mâmbu], became the Egyptian ankh or symbol of life.

Of course, among the Bântu people, an ngânga stands "vertically," and powerfully inside the community "Vee" [telama lwîmbangânga mu kânda], as the symbol of active life in the community.

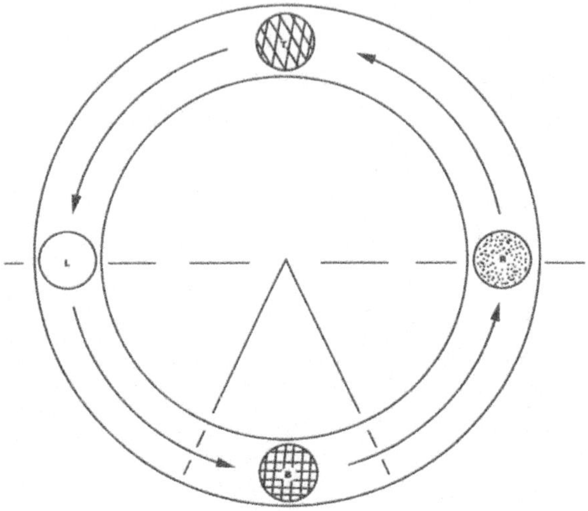

Figure 24.

From inside the "Vee" the human being [mûntu] comes to be [kala], and within the Vee he extinguishes [zima] as living energy. Therefore, the Vee in reality, is a living pyramid in constant motion, which follows the path of life and passes the four main points of demarcation of the cosmogram [dikenga], which in turn is symbolized by the flame of life inside the community circle. The closer one is to the center of this flame, whose "Vee" is the symbol, the healthier and more powerful one is. On the contrary, the more distant one is from this center, the weaker and less powerful one becomes. **(See figure 19).**

African people in Africa and Diaspora have lost their closeness to the center of the community cultural "Vee". The Bântu-Kôngo philosophy, whose "Vee" is only one of its most important aspects, teaches that the human being [mûntu plural bântu] is both a living-energy-being (spiritual being) and a physical being (matter). It can be said a "V-H being", i.e., he is a being [kadi/be] that stands vertically, i.e., he thinks-reasons-ponders, before he walks and acts to meet horizontally the challenges of the instinctive world; this is the horizontal world, which is the main ground to all learnings.

Walking horizontally is a process and a motion with one intention, which is going to learn from one's environment, the circle, for "knowledge is not in us; it is outside of us." We are only shelving machines, living computers, with the power to collect and shelve the information for future use, at will.[2] Horizontal motion [kilukôngolo], is especially a cognitive process [dingo-dingo dianzâyila]. Without this cognitive motion, the human being [mûntu] becomes powerless in his own environments, both inner and outer.

On the "V-H" ground, vertical-horizontal [Kintombayulu-Kilukôngolo], the human being [mûntu] has two planes for his motion/movement. On the horizontal plane he can move in four directions: forwards, backwards, leftwards and rightwards. Motions towards these four directions are for learning, i.e., collecting information (data)

---

2. Fu-Kiau: Lecture at the Carribean Cultural Center, N.Y. 1988; Harvard Univsity in Blk. Studies Dept. 1992; ASA Conference Pittsburg 1995.

to be shelved in his bank, the mind. But thanks to the vertical plane, he can walk into three more directions, of which one is critical to both his health and self-healing. The vertical plane allows him to walk downwards, upwards and for "perfect" health, true self-knowing and self-healing, walk innerwards.

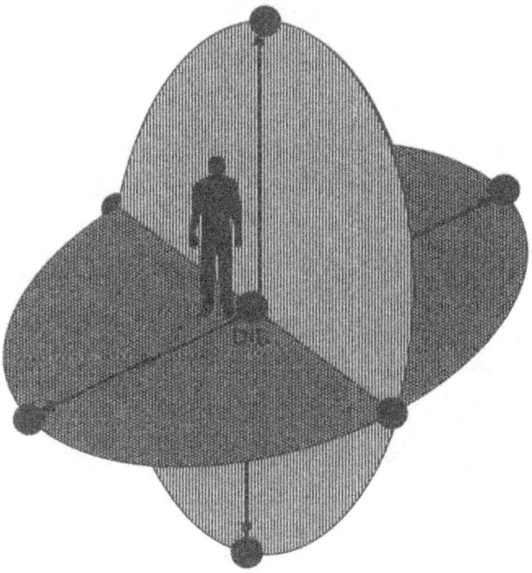

Figure 25.

The Bântu people, in their teaching, believe that the human being suffers mostly because of his lack of knowing how to walk towards this 7th direction, the innerwards direction. Their own words put it so perfectly well: Kani ka bwè, kana ku lumoso-ku lubakala-ku n'twâla-ku nima-mu zulu evo mu nsi ukwènda, vutukisa va didi i yând. (No matter what, you may walk leftwards, rightwards, forwards, backwards, upwards or downwards, you must come back to the core/center).

The human being is nothing unless he discovers how to walk towards the 7th direction, the center [didi], the inner world which represents the essence of his being [bukadi bwândi/bukadi bwa mbèlo ândi]. As such, one has to discover, or rediscover, this walk towards the 7th direction, not only for the sake of health and self-healing, but because it empowers one for self-knowing as well. It allows us to truly become "thinking-acting-beings" [kadi-biyîndulanga-mu-vânga], i.e., doers [vângi] because we are masters [ngânga] to ourselves.

But when the core of a body is oppressed, destroyed, polluted, corrupted, or raped, be it biological, societal, institutional or national, the body that envelops it is itself dead. The path that leads towards it, the 7th direction, is also wiped out. People become helpless. They lose their self-healing power and their order-giver-stimulus.

In this situation the body cannot be healed unless the "primitive" state of the core is restored. To do so is a process of cleansing its core, i.e., "depolluting" it. In other words it is learning the techniques of the curative "garbology" [kinzûdi kiandiakisina] which is a process of digging out the junk that prevents access to the core of the inner power.

The walk on the path towards the 7th direction is the key to all healings. To help one walk on this path is not only to empower him/her, but it is to restore him/her as a whole. It is to restore the self-healing power and turn on again the order-giver-stimulus.

The "Vee", teaches the Bântu-Kôngo philosophy, is both expandable and shrinkable. Through initiation [Ghânda/ Vânda, one learns how to widen

[Vôngisa/zibula] one's "V", the door of insight [vitu di-ambwèna]. If learning [longuka] is the process through which we widen our doors of insight, our individual as well as our collective "Vees", we narrow or destory them and ourselves at once through abuses such as drugs, mental imprisonment, food, profanity and ignorance

According to these teachings, which the Kôngo consider the first instructions and key principals [n'kîngu mi-angudi] to life, one has to focus on four main or essential "Vees". Each of the main "Vees" correspond to one specific point of demarcation on the Kôngo cosmogram [dikenga dia Kôngo] and its symbolic colour. These points of demarcation are: Musoni (yellow demarcation point), Kala (black demarcation point), Tukula (red demarcation point) and Luvèmba (white demarcation point). Furthermore, these points of demarcation, in Bântu-Kôngo thought, are the four greatest "suns" of all formation processes of change. The first (Musoni sun) is the sun of the "go order" [lutumu lwa mvangumunu] to all beginnings; the second (Kala sun) is the sun of all births; the third (Tukula sun) is the sun of maturity, leadership and creativity; the fourth (Luvemba sun) is the sun of the last and greatest change of all, death (Fu-Kiau, 1980).

Now that we have a clear idea about the Bântu-Kôngo cosmogram, its points of demarcation and its "suns" as well, let me present you a brief description of each one of the four main "Vees".

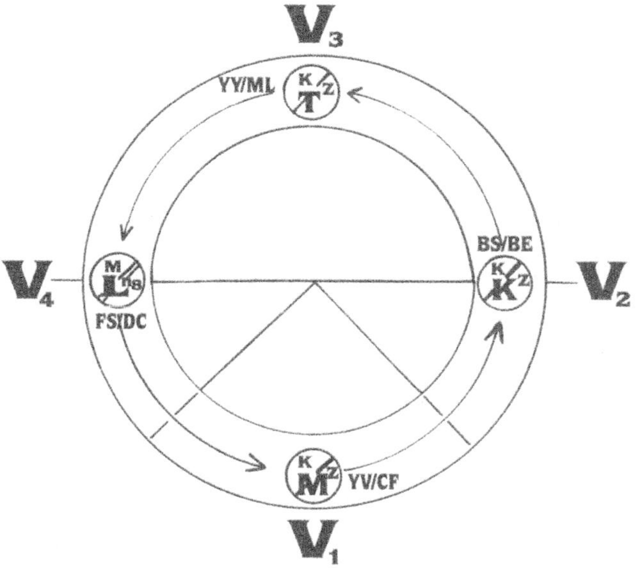

Figure 26.

1. The first, V1, is called Vângama, especially at the inititaion spot/institution [Kânga or Kôngo]. It is the formation process stage of life or Musoni stage. **(See figure 26a).**

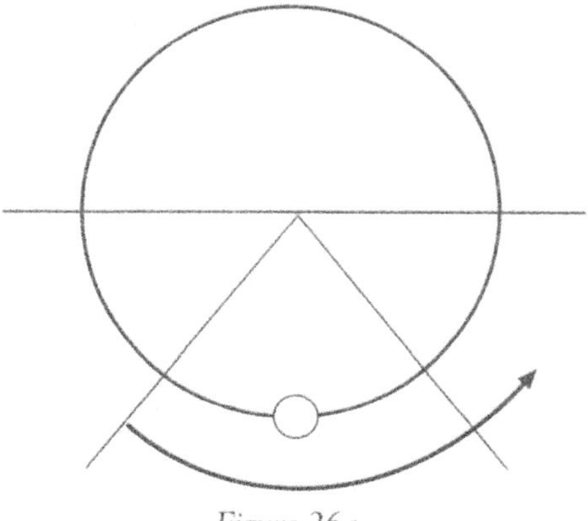

Figure 26a.

At this starting stage of the formation process [mvangu-munu] of biological life, all genetic codes [tambukusu] are imprinted [sonwa] into the future "living sun" to be, the child. The function of Vângama is accomplished under the conception action [yakwa].

In this sense, ideologically, we all get pregnant. And all pregnancies begin inside the "V1", the most fertile garden of all. During this vângama process, the being[be/kadi] in the formation process, turns into a breathing-being [vû-muni] in its first environment, the inner environment. The second key word in this stage vûmuni the breathing-being finds its root from the verb vûmuna, to breathe. It is the functioning process of all biological "motors", the heart. Formation of the breathing process "vângama mu vûmuna is the key to the V1 stage. With this breathing power [lèndo mu vûmuna] the inner development itself of the being to be [kadi/be] begins to accelerate in order to expand itself and its environment as well.

2. The second, "V2", is known as Vaika. It is the "V" that represents the existence stage of life or kala stage; to be, to exist, to rise. This Vee is the door into the physical world. Under this "V", "things" are born, rise up to the upper world [ku nseke] as "living" suns in the community, biologically or ideologically, have their birth at this stage under the Kala Sun. The function of Vaika from the inner to the outer environment is accomplished under the birth action [butuka]. **(See figure 26b)**.

During the "vaika-butuka" process, the body of the "living sun" rising in the upper world is empowered with a new sound-making energy. The new being [kadi kiampa] becomes

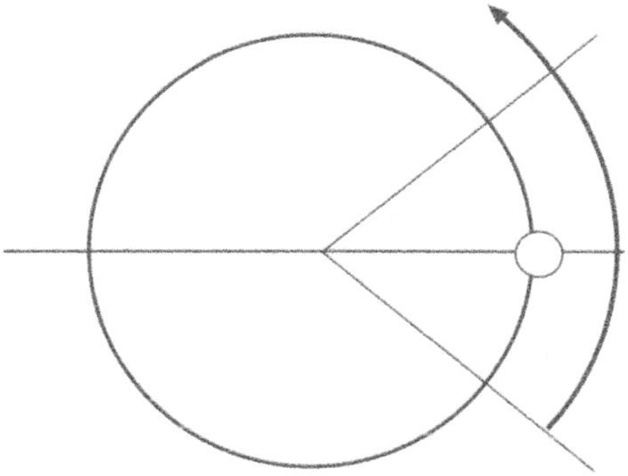

Figure 26b.

a speaking being [vovi]. This second key word to the V2, speaking being [vovi], finds its root from the verb "vova", to speak. Vova, to speak, is to code and decode, for the outside world, the universe, what is genetically coded/printed [sonwa] inside one's inner darkroom. It is not only to feed the ears of the world, but to fill with our waves (expressed energies) the cosmic voids. It is to hear and to be heard.

The butuka-vova is the process through which orders are given, received or rejected. Vova, speaking, gives us the mastery of being and/or of becoming. This second "Vee" is also known as the healing and cursing Vee; reviving and killing Vee [Vova sakumuni ye sîngi/fûmpudi ye fûmbudi]. It is the Vee that teaches about the power of words in and around us in life: Mâmbu makela, words are bullets, says a Kôngo saying.

3. The third "Vee", V3, is called Vânga, derived from the archaic word "ghânga" to perform, to do. This Vee, the most crucial in life, represents the stage of creativity and great deeds or tukula stage of the root verb kula, to mature, to master. **(See figure 26c)**.

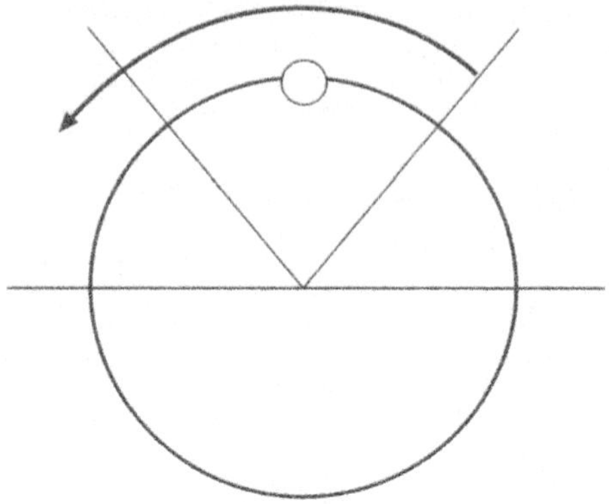

Figure 26c.

It is the symbol of the stage that is the most aspired to in the physical world. Inventions, great works of art, etc., are accomplished while one is passing through this zone of life. At this point one becomes an "ngânga", a master, a doer, a specialist in the community of doers. "Muna Kôngo: Vo kughânga ko, kudia ko"—In Kôngo society, if you don't do, you don't eat.[3] The Vânga function is accomplished by the kula, grow action, i.e., learning to "stand vertically" [telama lwîmbangânga] inside one's "V".

This Vee, the third, is a reversed pyramid. It occupies the position of verticality [kintombayulu], the direction of gods, power and leadership. People, institutions, societies and nations as well, enter and exist in this zone successfully, only if they stand on their own feet. One enters and stands up inside this Vee to become a doer/master [ngânga], to oneself first before becoming an ngânga to the community.

3. One cannot share or enjoy the community wealth unless he/she participates to accumulate it.

This Vee and the zone it occupies is the scale to all: our words, deeds, thoughts, movements, projects, meals, relationships, etc., and their impact on our health as individuals, institutions, societies and nations as well are weighed on the scale of the Vee.

To stand "well" inside this scaling Vee is to be able not only to master our lives, but to better know ourselves and our relationship positions with the rest of the universe as a whole.

4. The last or fourth Vee, V4, is Vûnda. This "V" represents the stage of the greatest change of all changes, death. This stage is known as Luvèmba stage. Under this stage one goes naturally or unnaturally into the process of dying or Vûnda, i.e., to rest, to extinguish, leave the physical world, to re-enter the world of living energy, which is the spiritual world, the ancestors' world. It is going in vacations [Kwènda ku mvûndulu]. In the process, one becomes either an n'kuyu, which means an ugly, imature, stunted [kuya] ancestor, or, the spiritually deified ancestor [mukulu/n'kulu]. The Vûnda function is completed under the fwa, die, action **(See figure 26d)**.

The "Vee" is not only a human experience, it is found everywhere in nature as well as in the universe. It is the most primitive form that emerged from the depth of the first matter, "the dark matter" [ndobe/piu], which is the "printing room" of all realities, not only visible and invisible, but material and immaterial as well. A "printing room" for realities that were and realities to come. It is the printing room inside where all great ideas, images and forms emerge to be impregnated in our minds. Thereafter, we create them as realities.

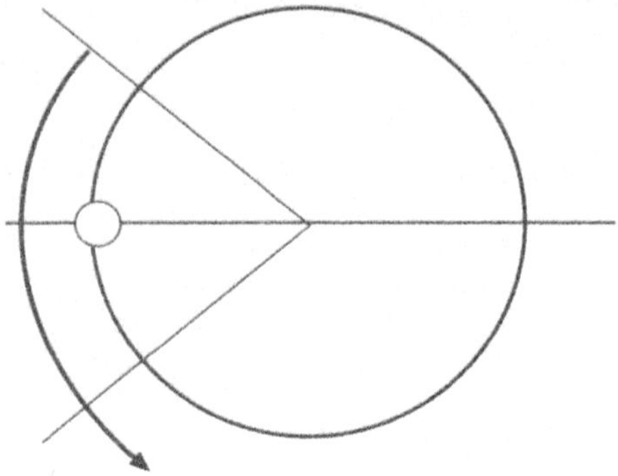

Figure 26d.

The "Vee" is a living energy ["V" i lêndo kiavûmuna] and, as such, it is the basis [fuma/sînsi] of the reproductive web of life [dingo-dingo diantûngila lukosi lwa môyo]. Under the "Vee" we greet our friends and loved ones. It is under these "meeting Vees" that love, lust and infatuation become a part of the human experience. It is also under these "meeting Vees" that friendships, partnerships and all kinds of relationshps are created among people, communities, institutions and nations as well.

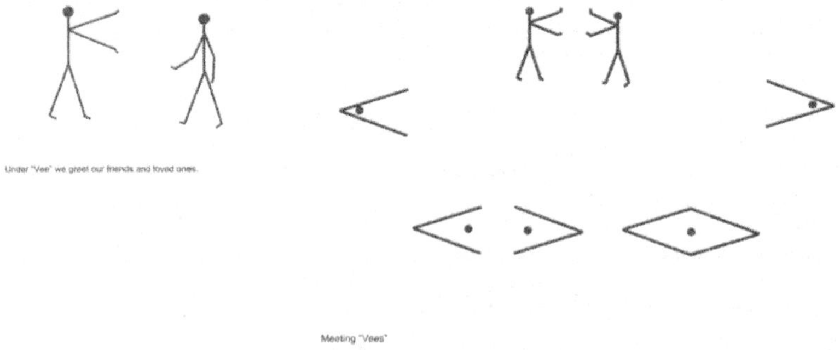

Figure 27.

When two "Vees" of opposite but attractive energies meet, they form a new body, a pattern in the form of a diamond, within which emerges a strong core of vitality [kimôyo], the seed of breath [vûmunu]. From this core-energy [didi dia ngolo], new lives, new products, new works of art and new organizations are born. In other words, these diamond-like cores can reproduce other "Vees" which at their turn meet other "Vees". It is the natural law of procreation, speech/language, creativity, motion, etc. A circle is an ensemble of many "Vees" in motion **[See figure 27a]**.

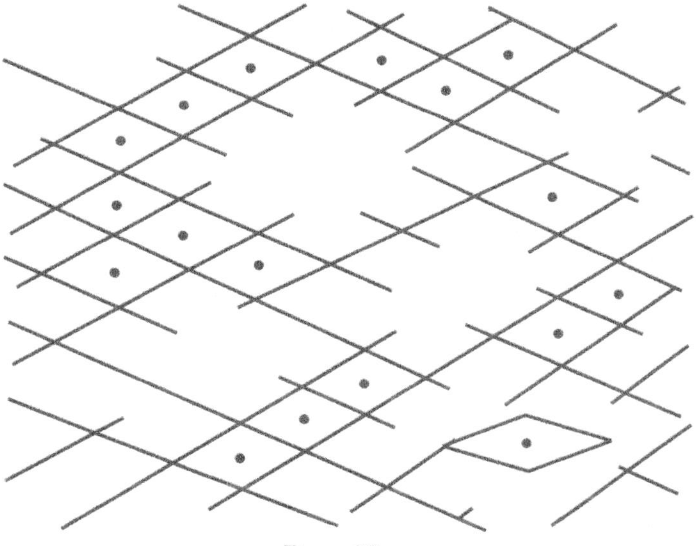

Figure 27a.

This diamond-like pattern, very common in Bântu industry of art and weaving, is a focus on life [môyo], its reproductive web, and its value among the Bântu people in particular, and among all African people in general. Velvets woven on the ground of this pattern became didactical tools used to teach the formation process of societies; these patterns are taught to the communities, the families and extended families. Western scholars of the African industry of art and weaving (visual art) were unable to explain these African iconographs. Their lack of knowledge about the Bântu world view, their cosmologies, and their vital concept of the "Vee" discussed here did not prepare them.

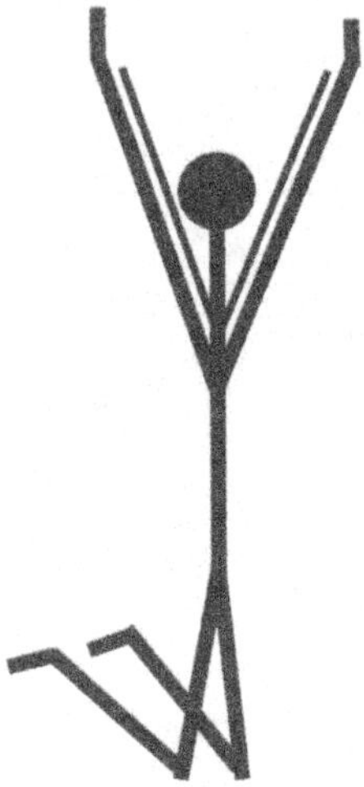

Figure 28.

Under the "Vee" we acknowledge our victories. Under the "Vee" we scream up for pain or joy. **(See figure 28a)**. Under the "V" we see what we see inside the field of our sight. Under the Vee's light we dig up into our past memories. Under the beam of the Vee emerging from the the dark matter [piu] that makes the creative vision possible, we rediscover lost details in our memories.

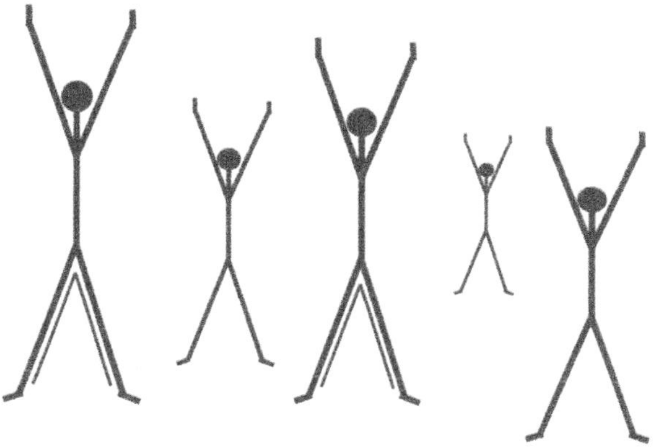

Under "Vee" we scream out for pain or joy.

Figure 28a.

Figure 29.

The "V" is not rare in nature. Many grasses grow up keeping their "V" form. Trees maintain this V form in their branch ramifications as they do keep their reverse "V" in foliage formation process. This most secret form of "V", the reverse Vee or pyramid is kept by most world mountains. **(See figure 29a)**. These mountains are true natural "dark rooms" inside which are hidden forces, powers, medicines and mysteries of all times. They hide the first and most powerful witnesses of the planetary formation process. These witnesses are made silent by the "divine" presense, the agent of all formation processes.

Trees keep the"Vee" form (branches and foliage).

Figure 29a.

Figure 30.

Thanks also to the Vee form of their bodies, birds, fish and animals can move fast in their given environment. Flowers themselves, the beauties of nature, are living "Vees". **(See figure 31a)**. Last, but not least, rivers themselves, from their sources, are also "Vees" flowing and serpenting in our forests and valleys.

Figure 31.

Flowers, the beauties of nature, themselves are living "Vees".

Figure 31a.

Have we not asked why our own best machines run or fly faster? Because they are, of course, made in forms of the "V". Also, because we cannot live ourselves outside of the "Vee", this fundamental truth is reflected on our own made machines, boats, canoes, trains, airplanes, etc.

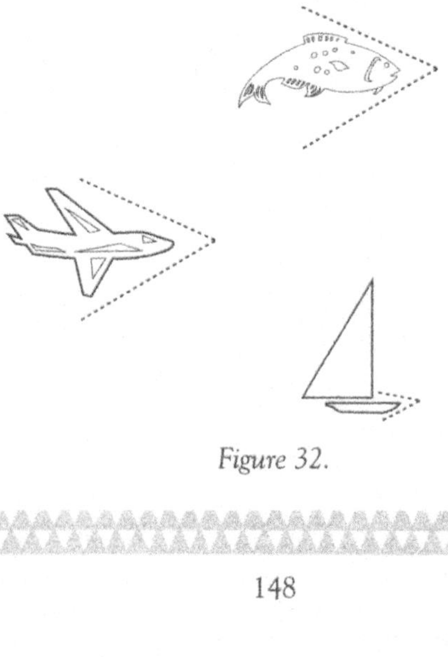

Figure 32.

The "Vee" is life and all its realities. It is the center of all existence. It is the chaos of all chaos. It is the center of balance [kinenga] for the human being [mûntu], his health and that of his community as well. It is the key to all aspects of simple life. It is the binding force to all: earth, plants, animals, birds, insects, reptiles and human beings as one by natural law. It is the Vee that differentiates human beings [mûntu] from the beast. The [mûntu] is fundamentally a "vertical being". He thinks and he is spiritual. Some people deny being spiritual, but I am afraid if they are not more spiritual than those who say they are. The beast, on the contrary, is a "horizontal being," a prostrated being that acts instinctively. Mûntu, by his behavior, can fall to the level of animals; but the animal cannot rise to the level of the vertically thinking being, the mûntu.

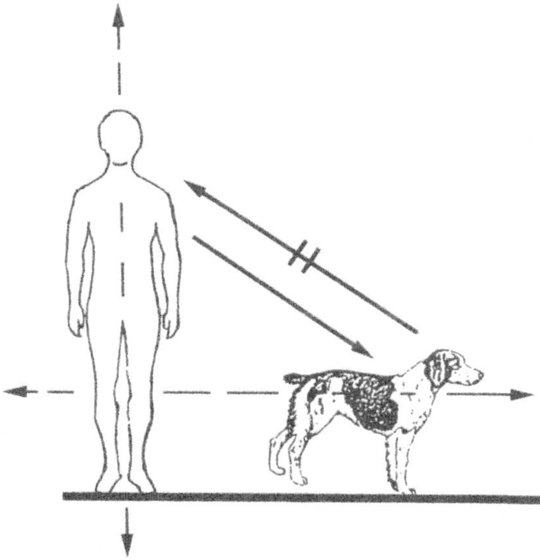

Figure 33.

Understanding the personal, collective, and cosmic "Vees" is a process of opening doors to new horizons which can allow one to see and accept things both seen and unseen, the way they are and not as one would like them to be. This is a spiritual channel through which a human can understand all his past, present and future masters [sîmbi], political or spiritual leaders, as humans first, then spiritual leaders. It is understanding that the KALA and ZIMA, the ON and OFF, the yin and yang, are not separate conceptual entities/realities; they both are a token of two sides in one process of motion and change. [Dingo-dingo dia minika ye nsobolo].

ANNEX

I. NDOZI—DREAMS

Bakwèndanga	Those who are departing
Ndozi	Dreams
Bèto	Ourselves
Ndozi	Dreams
Bakwîzanga	Those who are entering
Ndozi	Dreams
Ndozi	Dreams
Ndozi	Dreams
Ndozi ye ndozi	Dreams and dreams
Bakulu	The ancestors
Ndozi	Dreams
Bangânga	Initiated/specialists
Ndozi	Dreams
Biyînga	Non-initiated/laymen
Ndozi	Dreams
Ndozi	Dreams
Ndozi	Dreams
Ndozi ye ndozi	Dreams and dreams
Zuzi	Before yesterday
Ndozi	Dreams
Zôno	Yesterday

Ndozi	Dreams
Lumbu-ki	Today
Ndozi	Dreams
Mbazi	Tomorrow
Ndozi	Dreams
Ndozi	Dreams
Ndozi	Dreams
Ndozi ye ndozi	Dreams and dreams
Ndozi kaka	Always dreams
Kwakônsono	Everywhere
Bônso nkûmbu	Like name
Yeti lânda mûntu	Accompanying the owner
Bônso budîmbu	Like the glue
Lumbu biabio	All days
Mu luzîngu	In life
Ndozi	Dreams
Ndozi	Dreams
Ndozi ye ndozi	Dreams and dreams
Bâna	Kids
Ndozi	Dreams
Bambuta	Elders
Ndozi	Dreams
Mazoba	Idiots
Ndozi	Dreams
Bandwènga mpe	Scholars, too
Ndozi	Dreams
Ndozi	Dreams
Ndozi	Dreams
Ndozi ye ndozi	Dreams and dreams

Nga zèyi	Do you understand?
Makutèlanga ndozi	What dreams tell you
Mu diâmbu dia kânda diâku	Concerning your community
Mu diâmbu dia nsi âku	Concerning your country
Ndozi	Dreams
Ndozi	Dreams
Ndozi ye ndozi	Dreams and dreams
Mono vo	And I'm telling you
Lôtwa	Dream
Ye zâya maulôtwanga	And understand what you dream
Wavangikisa mo	For their realization
Mu kânda diâku	Within your community
Mu nsi âku	In your country
Lôtwa	Dream
Lôtwa	Dream
Lôtwa ye lôtwa	Dream and dream

II. KU NSEKE

Luzîngu ku nseke i:
Longwa ye longila
Tâmbula ye tambikisa
Zolwa ye zola
Tûmbwa ye tûmba
Katula ye katulwa
Dila ye dilwa
Mu soba…

IN THE PHYSICAL WORLD

Life in the physical world is:
To be taught and to teach
To receive and to give
To love and be loved
To be crowned and to crown
To dethrone and to be dethroned
To bury and to be buried
For change…

Smallest among thousands of works about Africa,
but I send you,
go, *African Cosmology of the Kongo-Bantu,*
talk about yourself to others
and be, a spark in the bush!
[kele-kele ku futa].

The author

Bibliography of Sources Cited

Balikci, A., 1970: *The Netsilik Eskimo*. Garden City, New York

Batsikama-ba-Mampuya, 1971: *Voici les Jagas*. ONRD. Kin/Zaire

De Cleene, 1946: "La Notion de propriete chez les populations matrilineales du Congo Belge", in Africa., Buxelles

K. Kia Bunseki, Fu-Kiau,

1994: Ntângu-Tându-Kolo: the Bântu Concept of Time in *Time in the Black Experience*, Adjaye, J.K. (ed). Greenwood Press.

1970: *Kindoki ou solution attendue*; Luyalungunu lwa Kumba, Luozi/Bas-Zaire

1969a: *N'kôngo ye nza yakun'zungidila/Le Mukongo et le mode qui l'entourait*. ONRD, Kin/Congo.

1969b: "Kwa nani zolele vova" (To whom are you speaking?), in *Moyo*, No. 9; Kin/Congo.

Unpublished works:

1978: *Makuku Matatu: les fondements culturels Kôngo*. (pp 450).

1975: *Ku Nènga: Verite sur les grandes initiations en Afrigque Centrale*. (pp 300).

1968: *Les proverbes Kôngo*.

Kajsa, E. 1972: *Power and prestige: the rise and fall of the Kôngo Kingdom.* Uppsala, Sweden.

Laman, K.B. 1918: *Laman Collection of Kôngo traditions.* (pp 20,000) in 10 microfilm rolls, Stockholm, Sweden.

Lemarchande, 1964: *Political awakening in the Belgian Congo.* Berkeley, Los Angeles.

MacGaffey, W., et al. 1974: *An Anthology of Kongo Religion,* Univ. of Kansas.

Muller, E.W., 1956: *Les droits de propriete chez les Mongo-Bokote.* Bruxelles, Belgium.

Munzele, Y., 1965: *Bakulu bèto ye dièla diâu.* Luyalungunu lwa Kûmba. Luozi/Bas-Zaire.

Obenga, Th., 1976: *La cuvette congolaise: les hommes et les structures.* Ed. Presence Africaine, Paris.

Read, H., 1864: *The Negro problem solved.* Mnemosyne Publishing Co. Inc., Miami, Florida.

Thompson, R.F., et al. 1981: *The Four Moments of the Sun:*

Kôngo Art in Two Worlds. National Gallery of Art, Washington.

Yabila, 1974: "Droit, revolution et vigilence revolutionaire" in *JIWE* No. 3, UNAZA, Lubumbashi/Zaire.

Young, C., 1965: *Introduction a la politique congolaise.* CRISP, Bruxelles, Belgium.

William, J.C., 1972: *Patrimonialism and political change in the Congo.*

Stanford University Press, Palo Alto, California.

About the Author

DR. FU-KIAU BUNSEKI is one of the most distinguished and insightful scholars of African culture. Born in Manianga, Congo, he was educated in both Western and African systems of thought.

He is initiated into three major traditional "secret societies", Lemba, Khimba and Kimpasi. These "secret societies" are in reality indigenous educational institutions. Lemba, is of particular relevance because it is the foundation for numerous african based religions and practices in the Americas, including Palo Mayombe in Cuba, Vodou Petro in Haiti, and Candomble Angola in Brazil; brought about through the transport of Central Africa's indigenous people to the new world during the slave trade.

While teaching in the city of Kinshasa, Dr. Fu-Kiau decided to return to his home, Manianga located in the countryside. There, he founded Luyalungunu Lwa Kumba-Nsi Institute, a pioneering education center dedicated to exploring and documenting traditional Kongo culture. His research and development work at the Institute laid bare the african philosophy of ancient Bantu educational institutions, which has had a significant. effect on major western scholars including Drs. Robert F. Thompson, John M. Janzen and Wyatt MacGaffey. Essentially, the cultural philosophy espoused by President Mobutu of Zaire on which he firmly established his national programme of Authenticite was based on the works of Fu-Kiau.

Fu-Kiau came to the United States to continue his education, and to educate Americans, particularly African Americans, about the complexity and depth of African philosophy. Since his arrival. he has done precisely that by means of various lectures and presentations. He has published numerous books and articles including *Kongo Cosmology, Kumina: A Kongo-based Tradition in the New World, Kindezi: The Kongo Art of Babysitting,* and *Self-Healing Power and Therapy, Old Teachings from Africa.* He Currently resides in Boston where he works as Director of Library Services at the Suffolk County House of Correction, and as Visiting Lecturer at the Tufts University Department of Anthropology and Sociology. He has also instituted two unique courses at the Suffolk County House of Correction: The Jail That Changed My Life and The African World and Culture. These courses are currently being turned into manuscripts for publication.

Dr. Fu-Kiau's academic background includes degrees in the areas of Cultural Anthropology (B.A.), School Administration (M.Ed.), Library Science (M.S.), and Education and Community Development (Ph.D.). An insightful scholar with a profound knowledge of Central African philosophy and Traditions, he is also a serious and committed educator with a wealth of experience, both in Africa and the United States. Dr. Fu-Kiau is a person of character, dedicated to the betterment of human-kind through traditional African ideas and means.

Made in the USA
Coppell, TX
08 April 2021

53415802R00094